thebus

CW00733473

The Bush Theatre
presents the European premiere of

2,000 Feet Away

by Anthony Weigh

11 June – 12 July 2008

Cast

in order of appearance

AG	**Ian Hart**
Boy	**Joe Ashman**
	Oliver Coopersmith
Byron/Resident	**Roger Sloman**
Nan	**Phyllis Logan**
Deputy	**Joseph Fiennes**
Woman/Manager	**Kirsty Bushell**
Waiter/18 Year Old	**Kevin Trainor**
Girl	**Charlotte Beaumont**
	Miranda Princi

Director	**Josie Rourke**
Designer	**Lucy Osborne**
Lighting Designer	**James Farncombe**
Sound Designer	**Emma Laxton**
Assistant Director	**Abigail Graham**
Deputy Production Manager	**Sam Craven-Griffiths**
Stage Managers	**Dawn Harvey**
	Amy Jones
Wardrobe Supervisor	**Alexie Kharibian**
Casting Director	**Janine Snape CDG**
Casting Assistant	**Tara Wilkinson**

2000 Feet Away received its European premiere on 11 June 2008.

Company

Joe Ashman (Boy)

Joe Ashman lives in Buckinghamshire and attends Sir Henry Floyd Grammar School and Stagecoach Leighton Buzzard.

Theatre includes *Chitty Chitty Bang Bang* (London Palladium), *The Cryptogram* (Donmar Warehouse), *The Sound of Music* (London Palladium), *Peter Pan* (Grove Theatre).

Film includes *The Golden Compass* (New Line Cinema

Charlotte Beaumont (Girl)

Theatre includes *Annie* (Watford Palace Theatre) and thirteen productions for Blag Youth Theatre.

Television includes *Scream* (Channel 4).

Kirsty Bushell (Woman/Manager)

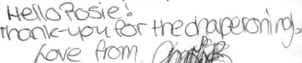

Kirsty trained at LAMDA.

Theatre includes *Testing the Echo* (Out of Joint), *Angels in America* (Lyric Hammersmith) for which she was nominated for the TMA and Scottish Critics Awards, *Twelfth Night* (RSC/Filter) *The Voysey Inheritance* (National Theatre), *The Comedy of Errors* (Sheffield Crucible), *Girl in the Goldfish Bowl* (Sheffield Crucible), *Don Juan* (Lyric Hammersmith), *Fen/Far Away* (Sheffield Crucible), *The Seagull* (Northampton Theatre), *Be My Baby* (Soho Theatre), *An Inspector Calls* (National Theatre/Garrick Theatre), *Two Gentlemen of Verona* (National Theatre), *Blue Heart* (Out of Joint).

Television includes *Pulling* (Silver River/BBC), *Talk To Me* (Company Pictures), *EastEnders* (BBC), *Midsomer Murders* (Bentley Productions), *Holby City* (BBC), *Family Man* (BBC), *Life Isn't All Ha Ha Hee Hee* (Hatrick), *Roger Roger* (BBC).

Film includes *Really* (Night for Day).

Oliver Coopersmith (Boy)

Theatre includes *Macbeth* (Regents Park Open Air Theatre), *The Cryptogram* (Donmar Warehouse).

Television includes *Hasbro Battleships* commercial (2am Films).

Film includes *It's Alive* (Nu Image).

Joseph Fiennes (Deputy)

Joseph trained at the Guildhall School of Music and Drama.

Theatre for the RSC includes *Les Enfants Du Paradis*, *As You Like It*, *Son of Man*, *The Herbal Bed*, *Troilus and Cressida*.

Other theatre includes *A Real Classy Affair* (Royal Court), *Edward II* (Sheffield Crucible), *Love's Labour's Lost* (National Theatre), *The Woman in Black* (Fortune Theatre), *A Month in the Country* (Albery), *A View From the Bridge* (Bristol Old Vic/West End), *Epitaph for George Dillon* (Comedy Theatre).

Television includes *Pretty Handsome* (20th Century Fox).

Film includes *Stealing Beauty* (Fiction), *Martha – Meet Frank, Daniel and Laurence* (Banshee), *Elizabeth* (Polygram), *Shakespeare in Love* (Universal), *Forever Mine* (Forever Mine), *Enemy at the Gate* (DOS), *Dust* (Alta Films), *Killing Me Softly* (MGM), *Leo* (Freewheel Productions), *The Great Raid* (Miramax), *The Merchant of Venice* (Spice Factory), *Luther* (Eikon), *Man To Man* (Vertigo), *Darwin Awards* (3 Ring Circus Films), *Running With Scissors* (Plan B Entertainment), *Goodbye Bafana* (Banana Films), *The Escapist* (Picture Farm), *Spring 41* (Opus Films), *Against The Current* (Ambush Entertainment).

Directorial credits include *The Spirit* (Russian World Studios).

Ian Hart (AG)

Theatre includes *The Homecoming* (The Gate Theatre, Dublin/ New York/The Comedy Theatre, Panton St).

Television includes *Dirt* (ABC/Touchstone), *Elizabeth: The Virgin Queen* (BBC), *The Return of Sherlock Holmes* (Tiger Aspect), *Eroica* (BBC), *The Hound of the Baskervilles* (Tiger Aspect).

Film includes *Morris: A Life with Bells On*, *A Cock and Bull Story* (Pluto Films), *Breakfast on Pluto* (Pluto Films), *Blind Flight* (Parralax), *Finding Neverland* (Miramax), *Harry Potter and the Sorcerer's Stone* (Warner Brothers), *Land and Freedom* (BIM), *The End of the Affair* (Columbia).

He has won Best Actor Award for *Blind Flight* at the Tribeca Film Festival 2004, Best Actor Award for *Aberdeen* at the Karlovy Vary Film Festival 2000, Best Supporting Actor Award (Venice Film Festival 1995) and Best Actor (Irish Times Theatre Award 2002) for *The Homecoming*.

Phyllis Logan (Nan)

Theatre includes *Richard III* (Crucible Theatre Sheffield), *Gaucho* (Hampstead Theatre Club), *Marvin's Room* (Hampstead Theatre Club/Comedy Theatre), *On The Edge* (Hampstead Theatre Club), *Minor Complications* (Royal Court Theatre).

Television includes *New Tricks V* (Wall to Wall), *The Royal* (ITV Productions), *Taggart – Trust* (SMG), *Honest* (Greenlit Rights), *Trial & Retribution* (La Plante Productons), *Richard Is My Boyfriend* (Windfall Films), *Heartbeat* (YTV), *Sea Of Souls* (BBC TV), *Spooks IV & V* (Kudos), four series of *Lovejoy* (Witzend Productions/BBC).

Film includes *Shooting Fish* (Gruber Brothers), *Secrets and Lies* (Thin Man Films), *Franz Kafka's It's a Wonderful Life* (BBC) and *Another Time, Another Place* (Associated-Rediffusion Television) for which she won a BAFTA.

Miranda Princi (Girl)

Television includes *Planet Cook* (CBBC).

Film includes *Blood and Chocolate* (Berrick Filmproduktion).

2000 Feet Away is Miranda's stage debut.

Roger Sloman (Byron/Resident)

Theatre for the RSC includes *Great Expectations*, *The Mandate*, *Much Ado About Nothing*, *Scenes From A Marriage*, *Merry Wives of Windsor* and for the National Theatre includes *Henry IV Parts I & II*, *Machinal*, *Richard II*, *Inadmissible Evidence*.

Other theatre includes *The Iceman Cometh* (Almeida), *My Night With Reg* (Criterion), *Numble Boy* (Northampton), *Henry V* (Royal Exchange), *Love's A Luxury* (Orange Tree), *A Chorus of Disapproval* (Scarborough), *Wholesome Glory* (Royal Court), *The Fosdyke Saga* (The Bush Theatre).

Television includes *Nuts In May* (BBC), *The Vicar of Dibley* (Brittom), *Foyle's War* (Greenlit Productions), *Touch Me I'm Karen Taylor* (Avalon Television), *Thieves Like Us*, *Mr Bean*, *Family Business*, *Grass*, *The Cazalet Chronicles* (BBC), *I Saw You* (Granada), *Pennies from Heaven* (BBC).

Film includes *Reds* (Paramount), *Beautiful People* (Tall Stories), *Chunky Monkey* (Head Gear Films), *Sorted*, *Tenth Kingdom* (Babelsberg Film und Fernsehen), *Beowulf* (Capitol Films), *Loch Ness* (Polygram), *The Young Indiana Jones Chronicles* (Amblin Entertainment)

Kevin Trainor (Waiter/18 Year Old)

Kevin trained at RADA.

Theatre for the RSC includes *Twelfth Night*, *Solstice*, *The Comedy of Errors*, *Eric la Rue*.

Other theatre includes *Bent* (Trafalgar Studios) and *Gladiator Games* (Stratford East).

Television includes *John Adams* (HBO), *Tripping Over* (Corner Stone Films), *The Catherine Tate Show* (BBC), *The Commander: Blackdog* (La Plante Productions), *Titanic: Birth Of a Legend* (Granada).

Film includes *Hellboy* (Columbia Tri Star), *The Hole* (Canal+).

James Farncombe (Lighting Designer)

Theatre for The Bush includes *Tinderbox*, *tHe dYsFUnCKshOnalZ!*, for which he was nominated for the Knight of Illumination Awards 2008, *Crooked* and *I Like Mine With A Kiss*.

A selection of recent work includes *Taking Care of Baby*, *Osama the Hero*, *Single Act* and *Life After Scandal* (Hampstead Theatre), *Breaking the Silence* and *Beast on the Moon* (Nottingham Playhouse), *Three Sisters* (Birmingham Rep), *Vincent in Brixton* and *The Glass Menagerie* (New Wolsey, Ipswich), *Be My Baby* (Stoke New Vic), *We That Are Left* (Watford Palace), *Touch Wood* (Stephen Joseph, Scarborough), *Blonde Bombshells of 1943* (Hampstead/TEG Productions). James lives in South London, on a hill . . .

For production photos and a full list of credits, please visit web.mac.com/jamesfarncombe

Abigail Graham (Assistant Director)

Abigail's directing career began with young people on housing estates in Hackney for Immediate Theatre. She is one of seven young directors on the Old Vic New Voices Programme 2006-7 and received the Company of Angel's Theatre Maker Award 2007-8.

Directing work includes: *Jack's Quest* (Junction, Cambridge/Pleasance, London), *The Boy and the Dog who Walked to the Moon* (Pleasance Courtyard, Edinburgh), *Lucy's Brief Guide on How to be Human* (The Old Vic), *Fear, Collective Energy* (The Apathists, Theatre 503), *The Crucible* (St. Luke's, Newcastle.)

Experience as an Assistant Director includes *Pub Quiz* (Northern Stage and regional tour, dir. Psyche Stott), *An Act of Love* (Old Vic 24 Hour Plays, dir. Edward Dick), *The Atheist* (Theatre 503), *Babel Junction* (Hackney Empire, dir. Suzanne Gorman)

Emma Laxton (Sound Designer)

Theatre for The Royal Court Theatre includes *That Face*, *Gone Too Far!*, *Catch*, *Scenes From The Back of Beyond*, *Woman and Scarecrow*, *The World's Biggest*

Diamond, *Incomplete And Random Acts of Kindness*, *My Name Is Rachel Corrie* (also Minetta Lane, New York/Galway Festival/Edinburgh Festival), *Bone*, *The Weather*, *Bear Hug*, *Terrorism*, *Food Chain*. West End theatre includes *That Face* (Duke Of York's), *My Name Is Rachel Corrie* (Playhouse Theatre).

Other theatre includes *Shoot/Get Treasure/Repeat* (National Theatre), *Europe* (Dundee Rep/Barbican Pit), *Other Hands* (Soho Theatre) *The Unthinkable* (Sheffield Theatres), *My Dad is a Birdman* (Young Vic), *The Gods Are Not To Blame* (Arcola Theatre), *Late Fragment* (Tristan Bates Theatre)

Lucy Osborne (Designer)

Lucy graduated from the Motley Theatre Design School.

Theatre for The Bush Theatre includes *Tinderbox, tHe dYsFUnCKshOnalZ!* and *Artefacts*.

Other theatre credits include *Be My Baby* (New Vic Theatre, Stoke), *Some Kind of Bliss* (Trafalgar Studios), *Rope* (Watermill Theatre), *Closer* (Northampton Theatre Royal), *Touch Wood* (Stephen Joseph Theatre), *Breaker Morant* (Edinburgh Festival 2007), *Ship of Fools* (set, Theatre 503), *The Long and the Short and the Tall* (Sheffield Lyceum and Tour), *Dr Faustus* (The Place), *Richard III* (Cambridge Arts Theatre), *The Tempest* (set, Box Clever national tour), *The Prayer Room* (Edinburgh International Festival/Birmingham Rep), *Flight Without End, Othello, Lysistrata* (LAMDA), *Season of Migration to the North* (RSC New Work Festival), *Almost Blue,* winner of the Oxford Samuel Beckett Trust Award (Riverside Studios), *The Unthinkable* (Sheffield Crucible Studio) and *Generation* (Gate Theatre, Notting Hill).

Josie Rourke (Director)

Josie is Artistic Director of The Bush Theatre. She trained as Resident Assistant Director at the Donmar Warehouse, was Trainee Associate Director at The Royal Court and was Associate Director of Sheffield Theatres.

Directing work includes *Tinderbox* and *How To Curse* (The Bush Theatre), *Loyal Women* and *Crazyblackmuthafuckin'-Self* (Royal Court), *The Cryptogram, World Music* and *Frame 312* (Donmar Warehouse), *Believe What You Will* and *King John* (RSC), *The Long and the Short and the Tall, Much Ado About Nothing, The Unthinkable, World Music* and *Kick for Touch* (Sheffield Theatres), *My Dad's a Birdman* (Young Vic) and *Romeo and Juliet* (Liverpool Playhouse). She has also directed the 24 Hour Plays at The Old Vic and on Broadway.

Anthony Weigh (Playwright)

Anthony is a graduate of the MPhil in Playwriting Studies at The University of Birmingham.

2,000 Feet Away is his first full length work and was developed whilst he was on attachment to the National Theatre Studio. It had its premiere at Belvoir Street Theatre, Sydney in November 2007.

He lives in London.

The Bush Theatre

'One of the most experienced prospectors of raw talent in Europe'
The Independent

The Bush is a world-famous home for new plays and an internationally-renowned champion of playwrights. We discover, nurture and produce the best new playwrights from the widest range of backgrounds, and present their work to the highest possible standards. We look for exciting new voices that tell contemporary stories with wit, style and passion and we champion work that is both provocative and entertaining.

The Bush has produced hundreds of ground-breaking premieres since its inception 36 years ago. The theatre produces up to eight productions of new plays a year, many of them Bush commissions, and hosts guest productions by leading companies and artists from all over the world.

The Bush is widely acclaimed as the seedbed for the best new playwrights, many of whom have gone on to become established names in the entertainment industry, including Steve Thompson, Jack Thorne, Amelia Bullmore, Dennis Kelly, Chloë Moss, David Eldridge, Stephen Poliakoff, Snoo Wilson, Terry Johnson, Kevin Elyot, Doug Lucie, Dusty Hughes, Sharman Macdonald, Billy Roche, Catherine Johnson, Philip Ridley, Richard Cameron, Jonathan Harvey, Conor McPherson, Joe Penhall, Helen Blakeman, Mark O'Rowe and Charlotte Jones. We also champion the introduction of new talent to the industry, whilst continuing to attract major acting and directing talents, including Richard Wilson, Nadim Sawalha, Bob Hoskins, Alan Rickman, Antony Sher, Stephen Rea, Frances Barber, Lindsay Duncan, Brian Cox, Kate Beckinsale, Patricia Hodge, Simon Callow, Alison Steadman, Jim Broadbent, Tim Roth, Jane Horrocks, Mike Leigh, Mike Figgis, Mike Newell, Victoria Wood and Julie Walters.

The Bush has won over one hundred awards, and developed an enviable reputation for touring its acclaimed productions nationally and internationally. Recent tours and transfers include the West End production of *Elling* (2007), the West End transfer and national tour of *Whipping it Up* (2007), a national tour of *Mammals* (2006), an international tour of *After The End* (2005–6), *adrenalin... heart* representing the UK in the Tokyo International Arts Festival (2004), the West End transfer (2002) and national tour (2004) of *The Glee Club*, a European tour of *Stitching* (2003) and Off-Broadway transfers of *Howie the Rookie* and *Resident Alien*. Film adaptations include *Beautiful Thing* and *Disco Pigs*.

The Bush Theatre provides a free script reading service, receiving over 1000 scripts through the post every year, and reading them all. This is one small part of a comprehensive Writers' Development Programme, which includes workshops, rehearsed readings, research bursaries, masterclasses, residencies and commissions. We have also launched a pilot scheme for an ambitious new education, training and professional development programme, **bush**futures, providing opportunities for different sectors of the community and professionals to access the expertise of Bush playwrights, directors, designers, technicians and actors, and to play an active role in influencing the future development of the theatre and its programme.

The Bush Theatre is proud of its reputation for artistic excellence, its friendly atmosphere, and its undisputed role as a major force in shaping the future of British theatre.

Josie Rourke
Artistic Director

bushfutures
building the theatre of tomorrow...

Projects this Summer

50 Ways to Leave Your Lover
By Leah Chillery, Ben Ellis, Stacey Gregg, Lucy Kirkwood and Ben Schiffer

Commissioned by Latitude Festival, five remarkable new playwrights have created *50 Ways to Leave Your Lover*: 50 break ups in 50 minutes, from the hilarious to the ridiculous. Inspired by true stories contributed by our audiences and developed by **bush**futures and The Bush's world-famous Literary Department, the show weaves individual voices with short scenes to create an evening that will strike a chord with anyone who's ever loved and left.

50 Ways to Leave Your Lover will tour to Oxford and Norwich before appearing at Latitude Festival and finishing with a week of performances at The Bush.

21-26 July, 8pm, £13 (£9 concs)

The Halo Project

Come and discover the secret life of Shepherds Bush.

Over five months, emerging performers from Hammersmith and Fulham have been working with playwright Simon Vinnicombe to develop a new play about Shepherds Bush, The Green and the part of London we call home.

28–30 August, 8pm

bushfutures, launched in 2007, is a ground breaking education, training and development programme that allows emerging theatre professionals and members of the local community to access the expertise of Bush playwrights, directors, designers, technicians and actors.

We are devoted to finding the Bush artists of tomorrow.

For more information go to
www.bushtheatre.co.uk/bushfutures.html

At The Bush Theatre

Artistic Director	**Josie Rourke**
General Manager	**Angela Bond**
Literary Manager	**Abigail Gonda**
Associate Director: **bush**futures	**Anthea Williams**
Finance Manager	**Dave Smith**
Development Manager	**Sophie Hussey**
Marketing Manager	**Dulcie Ball**
Production Manager	**Pauric Hackett**
Development Officer	**Sara-Jane Westrop**
Assistant Producer	**Caroline Dyott**
Literary Assistant	**Jane Fallowfield**
Box Office Supervisor	**Ian Poole**
Box Office Assistants	**Kirsty Cox, Clare Moss, Alicia Turrell**
Front of House Duty Managers	**Kellie Batchelor, Adrian Christopher, Alex Hern, Abigail Graham, Glenn Mortimer, Lois Tucker**
Duty Technicians	**Vivienne Clavering, Matthew Vile, Sara Macleod, Adrian Christopher, Jason Kirk, Rachel Newson , Mark Selby, Shelley Stace**
Associate Artists	**Tanya Burns, Chloe Emmerson, Richard Jordan, Paul Miller, Lucy Osborne**
Writer in Residence	**Jack Thorne**
Press Representative	**Ewan Thomson & Giles Cooper at Borkowski**
Marketing	**Ben Jefferies at Spark Arts Marketing**

The Bush Theatre
Shepherds Bush Green
London W12 8QD

Box Office: 020 7610 4224

www.bushtheatre.co.uk

The Alternative Theatre Company Ltd. (The Bush Theatre)
is a Registered Charity no. 270080

Company registration no. 1221968
VAT no. 228 3168 73

Be There At The Beginning

Our work identifying and nurturing writers is only made possible through the generous support of our Patrons and other donors. Thank you to all those who have supported us during the last year.

If you are interested in finding out how to be involved, visit the 'Support Us' section of our website, email development@bushtheatre.co.uk or call 020 7602 3703.

Lone Star
Gianni Alen-Buckley
Princess of Darkness
Catherine & Pierre Lagrange

Handful of Stars
Joe Hemani
Sarah Phelps

Glee Club
Anonymous
Judith Bollinger
Jim Broadbent
Clyde Cooper
David & Alexandra Emmerson
Sophie Fauchier
Albert & Lynn Fuss
Piers & Melanie Gibson
Tanny Gordon
Adam Kenwright
Jacky Lambert
Curtis Brown Group Ltd
Richard & Elizabeth Philipps
Alan Rickman
Paul & Jill Ruddock
John & Tita Shakeshaft
June Summerill
The Peter Wolff Theatre Trust

Beautiful Thing
Anonymous
Mrs Oonagh Berry
John Bottrill
Seana Brennan
Alan Brodie
Kate Brooke
David Brooks
Maggie Burrows
Clive Butler
Justin Coldwell
Jeremy Conway
Anna Donald
Mike Figgis
Alex Gammie
Vivien Goodwin
Sheila Hancock
David Hare
Lucy Heller
Francis & Mary-Lou Hussey
Virginia Ironside
The Violet Crème
Kim Lavery

Jeremy & Britta Lloyd
Laurie Marsh
Ligeia Marsh
Kirsty Mclaren
Michael McCoy
Tim McInnerny
& Annie Gosney
John Michie
David & Anita Miles
Mr & Mrs Philip Mould
John & Jacqui Pearson
Richard Philp
Mr & Mrs A Radcliffe
Wendy Rawson
John Reynolds
Caroline Robinson
David Pugh & Dafydd Rogers
Nadim Sawalha
Barry Serjent
Brian D Smith
Mrs Peter Templeton
Abigail Uden
Barrie & Roxanne Wilson

Rookies
Anonymous
Neil Adleman
Tony Allday
Ross Anderson
Pauline Asper Management
Mr & Mrs Badrichani
Constance Byam Shaw
Tanya Burns & Sally Crabb
Geraldine Caulfield
Nigel Clark
Alan Davidson
Joy Dean
Nina Drucker
Sally Godley
Miranda Greig
Peter Grundy
Sian Hansen
Andy Herrity
Mr G Hopkinson
Joyce Hytner, ACT IV
Robert Israel for Gordon & Co.
Peter James
Hardeep Kalsi
Casarotto Ramsay
& Associates Ltd
Robin Kermode

Ray Miles
Toby Moorcroft-Sayle Screen
Georgia Oetker
Mr & Mrs Malcolm Ogden
Julian & Amanda Platt
Radfin
Clare Rich
Mark Roberts
David Robinson
Councillor Minnie Scott
Russell
Martin Shenfield
John Trotter
Loveday Waymouth
Clare Williams
Alison Winter

Platinum Corporate Members
Anonymous

Silver Corporate Members
The Agency (London) Ltd
Harbottle & Lewis LLP
United Agents

Bronze Corporate Members
Act Productions Ltd
Artists Rights Group
Hat Trick Productions
Orion Management

Trust and Foundation Supporters
The John S Cohen Foundation
The Earls Court and Olympia Charitable Trust
The Ernest Cook Trust
Garfield Weston Foundation
The Girdlers' Company Charitable Trust
The John Thaw Foundation
The Kobler Trust
The Martin Bowley Charitable Trust
The Mercers' Company
The Royal Victoria Hall Charitable Trust
The Thistle Trust
The Vandervell Foundation
The Harold Hyam Wingate Foundation

Acknowledgements

The author would like to thank: Sebastian Born,
Chris Campbell, Purni Morell and the staff
and actors of the National Theatre Studio,
where the work was developed; Lyn Wallis,
Lee Lewis and the cast and crew of the original
production, at Belvoir Street Theatre, Sydney;
Katherine Thompson, Linda Mclean,
Nancy Harris, Polly Rowe and Beth Drenning.
Special thanks to Josie Rourke and Lucy Osborne
for their faith and the road trip. Finally,
thanks and gratitude to Peter Gerard May,
without whom . . .

Anthony Weigh
2,000 Feet Away

faber and faber

First published in 2008
by Faber and Faber Limited
3 Queen Square, London WC1N 3AU

Typeset by Country Setting, Kingsdown, Kent CT14 8ES
Printed in England by CPI Bookmarque, Croydon, Surrey

A CIP record for this book
is available from the British Library

ISBN 978-0-571-24261-0

2 4 6 8 10 9 7 5 3 1

Characters

A. G.

Boy

Byron

Nan

Deputy

Woman

Waiter

Eighteen-Year-Old Male

Resident

Manager

Girl

Child
(non-speaking)

*A long dash — indicates a beat of action
without words*

*A forward slash / indicates that the next
character's line begins to overlap at this point;
when indicated, a third character may also
break in at the same point*

*A full stop, as well as representing the end
of a sentence, can also be an incomplete
or interrupted thought*

Prologue

*Chicago. The Daniel F. and Ada L. Rice Building, Art
Institute of Chicago. The painting 'American Gothic' by
the Iowan artist Grant Wood – a 1930s realist painting
depicting a man with pitchfork standing in front of a
young woman. A weatherboard house with imitation
gothic attic window is in the background.*

A. G. Dare you to touch it.

Boy Dare you to die.

A. G. Why not?

Boy Why should I?

A. G. Not cos I asked you to?

Boy You stupid?
An alarm'd go.

A. G. Let's see.

He goes to touch the painting.

Boy Where's all the rest?

A. G. Rest aren't coming.

Boy Just you and me?

A. G. Isn't that neat?

Boy Spose.

A. G. I've wanted to show you this for a long time. (*The
painting.*)

Boy This?

A. G. You like it?

Boy Looks like shit.
  I could do just as good.

A. G. Probably could.
  You're a good drawer.

Boy When you seen my drawing?

A. G. I see you in art sometimes.

Boy I draw alright.
  I spose.

A. G. You draw great.
  You play the piano great too.

Boy You're an OK teacher.

A. G. Thank you.

Boy I spose.
  I mean . . .
  I don't wanna hurl every time I think of piano lessons.
  So, guess you're doing something right.

A. G. I've been teaching a long time.

Boy You're pretty old.

A. G. You think?

Boy Yeah.

A. G. How old you think I am?

Boy Twenty-five.
  At least.
  —
  That security guard's looking at us.

A. G. Is he?

Boy He's probably gay.

A. G. You think?

Boy That's why he's looking at us like that.

—

He her pa or what? (*The painting.*)

A. G. Could be her husband.

Boy Gotta be three times her age!

A. G. Sometimes younger people like spending time with older people.

Boy So the others not coming?

A. G. This is a very important painting.
Like someone put 'America the Beautiful' on canvas.

Boy What?

A. G. Beaverboard to be exact.

Boy Beavers.

He chuckles.

A. G. It's like a new kind of painting for a new kind of country.
That window's like windows they got in Europe.
But it's not from Europe.
It's from here.
The window's in a house that's here.

Boy Here like Chicago?

A. G. No. Eldon, Iowa.

Boy Where's Eldon, Iowa?

A. G. Iowa.

Boy Chicago rules!
Everywhere else is shit.

A. G. I'm from there. (*Eldon, Iowa.*)

Boy Sorry.

A. G. Used to walk to school past this old house every day.

Boy Must be old then. (*House, he means.*)

A. G. Pretty. (*Old, he means.*)

Boy He looks like a rabbit caught in head lamps.

A. G. He's protecting what's his.

Boy You know a lot about it.

A. G. It's of where I grew up.
I know people who look like these two.

Boy Can't say I'd be inclined to wanna know anyone who looked like them two.

A. G. Thanks.

Boy For what?

A. G. For coming with me.

Boy Rude of the others not to show.

A. G. Can I tell you a secret?

Boy Yeah.

A. G. I didn't want them to show.

Boy Don't you like them?

A. G. I like being here with you.
Do you mind me saying that?
I don't want to embarrass you.

Boy It's alright.

A. G. Can I tell you something?

Boy You're full of stuff, ain't you?

A. G. When you said you'd come I was really happy.

Boy If I came out with half the stuff you come out with I'd be even less popular than I already am.

A. G. I didn't have many friends either when I was your age.

Boy In Eldon, Iowa?

A. G. Uh-huh.
It's hard.
Not having friends.

Boy I got friends!

A. G. I thought . . .

Boy I got plenty!
We hang out and shit.
Better than coming and looking at stupid pictures.
No wonder you had no friends.

A. G. You're very perceptive.

Boy Shut up.

A. G. That's a compliment.

Boy Thanks then.

A. G. We could do this again.

Boy I don't like it much.

A. G. We could do something else.

Boy Like what?

A. G. We could go somewhere and eat.
Get a burger.

Boy What sort of burger?

A. G. Cheese?
Whatever you want.

Boy Maybe.

A. G. I could get you a Blizzard.
   You like Blizzards?

Boy Not much.

A. G. I love them.
   Got a real sweet tooth.
   Got to have them without the nuts though.
   I'm allergic.
   I had one once when I was a kid.

Boy / In Iowa?

A. G. (*overlapping*) With the nuts.
   My tongue swelled up like a salted slug.
   I can have them now but I gotta have them without
the nuts.
   I'm allergic.
   I'm talking shit.

   Boy giggles.

I always talk shit when I'm nervous.

Boy What you nervous about?

A. G. That you won't say you'll go out . . . come out
with me again.
   You gonna say you'll come out again?

Boy Maybe, alright?

A. G. I wouldn't normally get someone like you.

Boy Get?

A. G. Go out with.

Boy You should stick to piano.
   When you talk about other stuff / it just sounds fucked
up.

A. G. (*overlapping*) You're right, I know.

Boy I'm not gay.

A. G. / I know that.

Boy (*overlapping*) I just.
 I thought this might be something . . .
 Stupid though.
 Stupid painting.

A. G. Why don't you give that stupid painting a good whack.
 For me.
 —

Boy I'm not gonna! /
 I'm not gonna go out with you again either.
 I hate Blizzards.

A. G. (*overlapping*) Keep your voice . . .
 Please don't . . .
 I didn't mean to . . .

Boy / Alright.
 Calm down.
 Don't go and start crying or something.

A. G. (*overlapping*) Please.
 I'm . . .
 I'm sorry.
 I should go.

 And as he does.

Boy Wait!
 —
 Sometimes.

 A.G. turns around.

At night.

I go out on the street and go to kids' houses down the street.

There's lots of kids in my street.

And I try their locks and stuff on their back doors and try and get in to see them.

A. G. You ever get in?

Boy Nope.

A. G. What would you do if you got in?

Boy Go to their bedrooms maybe.
Watch them sleep maybe.
Stick a brick through their skulls.
Get into bed with them.
Maybe.
—

I'm just talking shit!
You gotta cigarette?

A. G. We can't smoke in here.

Boy You got one, though?

A. G. Yeah.

Suddenly the boy slaps the painting.
An alarm rings.

Boy Told you alarm'd go!

A. G. Come on!

They run out of the gallery together.
The painting.
The alarm.
Black.

A Piece of Paper

Eldon, Iowa. A kitchen. Nan and Byron are dressed like the characters from Grant Wood's 'American Gothic'. The sound of a piano playing scales in another room.

Byron Saw them boys.

Nan Boys?

Byron Saw them.

Nan Which?

Byron Them.

Nan More than one?

Byron Seem so.
  A gang.

Nan A gang?

Byron Three or seven or so.

Nan Three's no gang.

Byron Seven then.

Nan Seven now.

Byron Running off.
  With my own eyes.

Nan Boys run.

Byron You gonna fix that curl?

Nan What?

Byron Girl from Co-op's entering.

Nan So?

Byron So.
  She's got a curl is so.

Nan Girl from Co-op's a brunette.

Byron Not losing for want of a curl.

Nan Man from the Go Through's entering his pigs.

Byron Pigs!

Nan Dressed up.

Byron Defiles the tradition.

Nan We're too old this year.

Byron You seen the painting?

Nan You're too old.

Byron I'm as old as him.

Nan Older.
  Much.

Byron State Senator's coming to hand the prize.

Nan Nice to give someone else a year.
  Good to share it around.
  Otherwise people will start saying things.
  At the checkout at the Go Through.
  We won eleven years in a row.

Byron No one's saying things.
  You gonna fix that curl?

Nan Won't stay.
  Time to give someone else a year.

  A knock at the door.

Byron Where's that brooch?

Nan Inside.

Byron Is it going to walk out here and pin itself on of its
own accord?

He goes to get it.

If I see those boys.

Nan Boy.

Byron Boys.
And it's twelve.

Nan Twelve?

Byron The competition.
It's not eleven.
It's twelve.
We won it twelve times.

Nan That's what I said.
Twelve.

Byron It's open! (*The door.*)

Deputy comes in holding a plastic bag at arm's length.

Deputy This yours?

Byron That look like mine?

Deputy On the doorstep like UPS.

Byron Not like any UPS I know.

Deputy Stinks. (*The bag.*)

Nan You eaten?

Deputy I had doughnuts at Jerry's.

Nan You and those doughnuts.

Deputy Not my fault.
He puts something in them.

Nan Never changes his oil.

He's been down there as long as I can remember and he's still cooking those donuts in the same oil as when Johnson was President.

Deputy You two look a treat.

Nan He's worried about my curl.

Byron Girl from the Co-op's entering.

Deputy Girl from Co-op's a brunette.

Nan That's what I said.

Byron State Senator's coming down to hand out the prizes.

Deputy There's a crowd down there already.
They were up half the night re-doing the banner.
Someone spelt 'Gothic Festival' with a 'z'.

Nan You gotta eat something.
Sit down.

Deputy This yours then? (*The bag.*)

Byron That's a bag of shit.

Nan Byron!

Deputy This your bag of shit then?

Byron I look like I shit in a bag?
I look like some old colostomy boy to you?

Deputy You wanna . . .? (*Take it?*)

Byron Besides.
It's boy's shit.

Deputy Shit's shit.

Nan You gonna . . .? (*To Byron.*)

Byron grabs the bag from the deputy.
He takes it into the next room.

16

Nan He thinks there's a gang of them.
   He thinks he's seen them.

   The piano stops playing.

Byron (*off*) Delivery for you.

Nan He's nervous is all.

   Byron comes back on without the bag.
      The piano starts playing.

Byron I'm gonna use that piano for firewood.

Nan I'm fixing him some food.

Deputy You got nothing to be nervous about, you know.
   Some of the earliest pictures in my head are of the two
of you at that Gothic Day Festival standing dressed
up out the front of that old house looking like the folks
from that painting and being handed the prize.
   It's part of how things are.

Byron Listen to the philosopher there.

Deputy I know how things are meant to be.

Nan I told him we should let someone else win this year.
   You don't want to get talked about in the line at the
Go Through.

Deputy No one's talking.

Nan I'm just saying . . .

Deputy Everyone talks to me and no one's talking.

Byron You know so much, what you know about that
gang who been shitting on our front stoop?
   You know much about them?

Deputy I've seen some kids.

Byron See?

Nan He says he saw a gang. (*Byron did.*)

Deputy I saw a few.

Byron Seven.
  There were seven.

Deputy There might have been seven or nine or so.

Byron See?
  Seven or nine or so.
  (*Disparaging.*) Three.
  A gang.
  I said so.
  What're you going to do about them?

Deputy They're kids.

Byron How'd you like if I came down to the station and shat on your front stoop?

Nan They're just having fun with us.

Byron You know what value is?

Deputy Sure I know.

Byron You see that plate?

Deputy This?

Byron That plate you're eating off of?
  You know who gave us that plate?

Deputy I . . .

Byron The mayor was the one who gave us that plate.
  Must have been when we won . . . what . . .?

Nan Fifth time.

Byron Fifth or sixth time we won the competition the mayor gave us this plate.
  You know what that means?

Deputy Means you look like the folks in that old painting.

Byron Means we are valued here.
  You know what value is?

Deputy Sure I do.

Byron This is a symbol for value.

Nan Let him eat.

Byron You know what a symbol is?

Deputy Sure.

Byron Eagle. America. Cross. Church. Plate. Value.
  Symbols.

Deputy It's a fine plate.

Byron You bet your life on it.
  A finer plate than you eat off of at home I'll bet.

Nan Not much use giving a plate when you've little to
put on it.

Byron It's the symbol that's at issue here.
  We are valued here.
  We've got plates and spoons and cups and table mats
and a fine set of sundae glasses to prove it.
  And those kids are coming here and fouling on our
stoop and disrespecting the value that we've got here.

Deputy They're just being kids now.

Byron What are you going to do about it?

Nan You want more syrup there?

Deputy You spare it?

Nan Got enough to flood a desert.
  He's always had a sweet tooth.

Deputy He?

Nan Him.
  In there. (*The piano player.*)

Deputy Plays that piano good.

Nan Syrup on everything.

Byron I hate sweet.

Nan Lucky I'm not offering.

Byron You just here to eat our food then?

Deputy Not my fault if folks in this town trying to fat me up like some calf you fixing to kill.

Byron Like some old tom cat going door to door making out he hasn't eaten, more like.

Deputy I said I'd eaten.

Nan You going to the Festival with anyone now?

Deputy I'm working.

Nan Plenty of nice girls would jump.

Deputy They wouldn't.

Nan That's what folks say.

Deputy No one's saying that.
  I'd know.

Nan There's plenty would jump.

Deputy Could fool me.

Nan I'd jump if I were thirty years younger / than I am.

Byron (*overlapping*) Listen to it.

Deputy You give me heartburn.

Byron That's the syrup.

Nan Hot out then?

Deputy It's August.

Nan All month.

Deputy I can give you a ride.

Nan We got a car.

Deputy I can put the siren on.

Nan Bet that old State Senator's got a police escort.

Deputy Bet he does.

Byron I don't care if I turn to dust waiting.
　　You two can go on talking syrup and police escorts.
　　I want to know what it is you're proposing to do to stop those boys from shitting in plastic bags and leaving them on my stoop!
　　That's all!

The Deputy puts down his knife and fork and takes out a piece of paper and puts it on the table.
　　He continues eating.
　　A cow with its cud.

Deputy That syrup Canadian?

Nan I don't think so.

Deputy It's good.

Nan Have some more.
　　I'm itching like a dog in hay.

Deputy That old dress.

Nan Spose.

Deputy Worth it when that state senator hands you the prize.

Nan Hope it's not another plate.

Byron snatches up the piece of paper and reads.

—

He puts it back on the table.

Byron About time.

—

(*To Nan.*) You gonna get that brooch then?

Nan There's a piece of paper on the table.

Byron (*to Deputy*) Bout time you started to act like you had a job and showed up here.

Deputy I couldn't do anything till I was told to.

Nan What's it about? (*The paper.*)

Deputy About?

Nan The paper.

Deputy Safety.
  I spose.

Byron Don't you forget that brooch.

Nan Safety? (*She picks up the paper.*)
  I don't see anything on here about safety.
  You see anything on here about safety?

Byron I see a dress without a brooch.

Nan What's all this about?

Byron (*to Deputy*) Fella from Go Through's putting in his pigs dressed up.

Deputy For a lark.

Byron Ought a be a law against it.

Deputy For a chuckle.

Byron Defiles the meaning.

Nan Plenty of jargon and words I don't recognise, but nothing about safety.
  You see anything about safety on this?

Byron You get that cameo brooch.

Nan He put this paper down here.
  Says it's about safety.
  You see that word here?
  For it to be about a thing you'd need to see it written down.
  The word.
  Look!

Byron Eviction notice!

Deputy Don't shoot the messenger is all.

Nan Who's getting evicted?

Byron Him.

Nan Him?

Byron In there.

Nan Him in there?

Byron Get that brooch.
  I won't be beat by a pig.

Nan He's getting evicted?

Deputy I just got told to bring it.

Nan Who would tell you to do such a thing?

Deputy It's the law.

Nan And you're the law.

Deputy I'm the Deputy.

Byron You know the law.

Nan Don't believe I do.

Byron You know the law.

Nan Don't believe I do.

Byron Named after that little Girl from up in Des Moines.

Deputy Cute as a button.
  Saw her picture on the news.

Byron Good at sports.
  Spitting image of her mother.
  Found her stuck under a rotten log in the Oskaloosa
Reservoir.
  Fella had done all kinds of stuff to her.
  Had a time telling her from the log they say.
  That true?

Deputy That's what I heard.

Nan What's this got to do with us?

Deputy Don't shoot the messenger is all I'm saying.

Nan You're crazy.
  Coming here with pieces of paper and talking eviction
and shooting messengers and you telling me about poor
girls in reservoirs.
  Is this a joke?

Deputy Don't wanna be late for that judging.

Nan I'm confused.

Deputy They just told me to bring it.

Nan Who's 'they' for Christ's?!

Byron You get in and get that brooch now.

Nan What's this law got to do with us?
  —

Deputy You got a school at the bottom of the road is the
thing.

Nan So?

Deputy So that's the thing, see?

Nan Been there forty years.

24

Deputy Well, school and him can't live in the same street, see?

Nan Have done most of their lives.

Deputy Law's brand new.
    Schools. Daycare places. Parks. Playgrounds.
Churches. Bus stops –

Nan What's he done?
    ——
    You deaf?
    ——
    What's he done that he can't live alongside an old school?

Byron I'm gonna get that brooch.

    He goes off.
        Piano stops.

Deputy Don't look at me.

Nan Your daddy always looked good in his uniform.

Deputy He did.

Nan You've got a button missing.
    You look like . . .
    Like some sort of goldfish standing there.
    Just looking.
    Make me want to be ill.

    Byron comes in with a brooch.

Byron Put it on.

Nan I was saying how good his daddy looked in a uniform.

Byron No one better.

Deputy You gonna find that those boys stop coming around.

Nan Which boys?

Deputy The gang of them.

Nan Why is that?

Deputy I'm just saying is all.

Nan You saying that by having him evicted that those boys would stop fouling our stoop?

Deputy Probably.
  Is what I'm saying.
  I'm not stupid.
  These things can be.
  I'm not a goldfish.
  These things are connected.
  See?
  You want them to stop fouling?
  Then.
  This should do it.
  I reckon.

Byron He's got a job to do.

Nan What if he doesn't go? (*The piano player.*)

Deputy He doesn't want to do that.

Nan Why not?

Deputy Might get ugly.

Nan This pretty ugly.

Deputy This?
  This just what we got to do.

Nan What if, though?

Deputy Then they'd come here and remove him.
  By force.
  I spose.

Nan There's that 'they' again.

Deputy Us.
We.

Byron Am I going to have to pin that thing on for you?
(*He does.*)

Nan Where's he going to go then?

Deputy I just got told to serve the notice.

Nan If someone has no home to sleep in?
There's that old festy smelling man who camps out in town.
He going to end up like him?

The piano starts to play a tune.

Is he?
Kids spitting on him and stubbing out cigarette butts on his head?

Deputy Folks got to be safe in their houses.
That's the thing.
Kids got to be safe at school.

Byron You make your bed.
You lie down in it.

Nan You?
—
You?

Byron He.

Deputy Some of them have gone to the shelter on Oak.

Nan Them?

Deputy But there's that child-minding facility on the corner of Elm.

Nan Then where they go?

Byron Look at me when I'm trying to pin this on. /
Don't want to open a vein.

Deputy (*overlapping*) One or two tried the Samaritans on Cleeves.

Nan Tried?

Deputy There's that park on Cleeves, though.

Byron Nice park, too.

Deputy Some've been sleeping at the station.

Nan Where do they sleep at the station?

Deputy Cells.

Nan Cells?

Deputy Not like they're in jail or anything.
We leave the doors open.

Nan Doors?

Deputy We've always got one or two of them hanging out down there.
Get them to stuff envelopes.

Nan Stuffing envelopes?

Deputy Some checking into the Motel 6.

Nan On the highway?

Deputy Or the Laz-y-By.

Byron Met a fella stayed there once.
Said towels weren't clean.

Deputy Ced-Rel Motel's out there too.

Nan That's the middle of nowhere.

Deputy That's the point.
No schools or parks or –

Nan You seen him?

Deputy Him?

Nan In there?

Deputy Sure I have.

Nan You talked to him?

Deputy Once or twice.
Seemed nice enough.

Nan He teaches, you know.

Byron Taught.

Nan The piano.
He could give you lessons.

Deputy I don't go in for music.

Nan gives little scream.

Byron Then hold still!

Nan Did you draw blood?

Byron Hold still or do it yourself!
Can't see a thing without my –
Hold still, I said!

He pricks himself.

Damn it!
You do it!
Ugly thing!
(*To Deputy.*) Bout time you acted like a Deputy and
did your job!
(*To Nan.*) You wanna stop the talking at the 'Go
Through'? /
You wanna stop the talking?
Then you let him do his job.
House smelled like ten kinds of shit since he came back
and it's not cos of those boys neither . . .

Nan (*overlapping*) He said there was none.
You said no one was talking.
I can't smell anything.

Deputy (*also overlapping*)) I couldn't do anything until they said do something.

Byron . . . The thing is.
Your children think that it stays their house for ever.
That they've got the right just to come home.
That they've got that right for ever.
Well, they don't.

Nan You said it was alright.
You said he could come home.

Byron Well, it's not his home anymore.
Not now with this law and a school at the end of the street.

Nan That school's always been there.

Byron (*to Deputy*) And you took your time.

Deputy I couldn't.

Byron Should have sold that piano when we had the chance.
Make good wood for something useful.
I'm in the car.

He goes.

Nan This competition is very important to him.

Deputy He's got nothing to worry about.
You two the spitting image.

Nan I suppose we are.

Deputy Thing is.
I've gotta put this in his hand.

Nan Whose?

Deputy His.
  In there.

Nan He's got nice hands.

Deputy It's how it works.
  It won't take me more than a minute.

  *She pushes a plate from the table (or perhaps she is
  holding it).*
    It smashes on the ground.

Nan We better get going.
  Don't want him being late down there for that judging.
  There'd be hell.

Deputy This won't take a minute.

Nan You wanna take some of that syrup with you?

Deputy You spare any?

Nan Help yourself.
  We've got gallons.
  He's got a sweet tooth. (*Indicating the pianist.*)
  Has it on everything.
  Hot cakes to cantaloupe.
  Steak if he could.
  No need of it now.
  Old boy and me.
  We don't care for sweet.

  She leaves.
    Deputy picks up the piece of paper.
    He listens to the piano.
    Black.

A Signature

Eldon, Iowa. Police station. A counter. A. G. sits on a metal folding chair in the back of the room with a small bag. Maybe he's stuffing envelopes. A Woman has a wad of papers and a brown paper bag of doughnuts.

Woman He drives slow.

That fella does.

Past the school.

Past the girls.
On the playing fields.
Doing callisthenics.

Driving slow past the girls doing callisthenics.

Deputy He doing callisthenics?

Woman You kidding me?

Deputy It's a joke.

Woman Funny.

Deputy You gotta laugh.

Woman No I don't.

Deputy A man driving and doing callisthenics.

Woman He's driving.
That fella is.
The girls are the ones doing callisthenics.

Deputy I'm not stupid.
  It's a joke.
  Not a crime to drive slow.

Woman Should be.

Deputy If he were driving fast now . . .

Woman We're not sleeping is all.

Deputy You should sleep.

Woman Well, we're not is what I'm talking about.
  And we're not the only ones.

Deputy No call not to sleep.

Woman He lives at the bottom of the street.

Deputy We know where he lives.

Woman Everyone knows what's what with him.

Deputy Just living there's not doing any harm.

Woman He drives slow past the girls doing callisthenics.

Deputy Just living and driving is no harm.

Woman You got kids?

Deputy You know I don't.

Woman You don't sleep when you got kids.

Deputy Should try warmed-up milk.

Woman Is that a joke again?

Deputy Helps you sleep is all.

Woman I've seen him.

Deputy You have?

Woman My husband has.

Deputy He has?

Woman His friend did.
Driving slow.
He'll get killed.

Deputy He better not.

Woman Can't say I'd blame . . .

Deputy Murder's against the law.

Woman My husband's not sleeping.
The thought of it.

Deputy Tell him not to think then.

Woman Haven't seen you in church lately.

Deputy I've been to church.

Woman Lately.

Deputy Lately I've been.

Woman Lots of pretty young things at the church.

Deputy So?

Woman So, is all I'm saying.
Big thing like you.

Deputy Routine's the key to sleep.
Get in the routine of doing the same thing every night
and pretty soon your body knows that the routine means
that it's time for sleep.
Like me it's: TV off, trash out, feed cats, teeth, lights
out.
I'm asleep before my head hits the pillow.

Woman You still feeding them cats?

Deputy Someone's got to.

Woman How many you got now?

Deputy Eight.

Woman Eight?

Deputy Twenty-four or so.
   Give or take.

Woman Should be taken and drowned in a bag.
   Pissing on people's yards.
   (*To A.G.*) You got a yard?
   Hey.

A. G. Pardon me?

Woman Cats piss on your yard?

A. G. I live with my parents.

Woman Your folks got a yard?

A. G. Not much of a one.

Woman Lucky.
   Cats piss on it if you do.

Deputy Cats are alright.

Woman Alright until they start pissing on your yard.

Deputy Feeding them is not doing any harm is all.

Woman No harm to you.
   I'm there.
   Lying awake.
   In the night.
   Smelling cats pissing on my yard.

Deputy Need a routine is what I'm saying and you fall in straight to sleep.

Woman Not knowing that that fella's at the end of the road we won't.
   Have a doughnut.

Deputy Rather not.

Woman Why not?

Deputy Trying not to is all.

Woman You on a diet?

Deputy No.

Woman So have one.

Deputy Don't wanna get fat.

Woman You on a diet then?

Deputy Just not eating doughnuts.

Woman Don't you like them?

Deputy I love them.

Woman Then have one then.

Deputy Rather not.

Woman (*to A. G.*) You wanna doughnut?

A. G. What?

Woman Help yourself if you want one.

He does.

A. G. Thank you.

Woman You got nice hands.

A. G. Thank you.

Woman Hasn't he got nice hands?

Deputy What?

—

Woman You gotta sign this, then.

She thrusts the wad of papers at him.

Deputy What's this?

Woman If you're not going to do anything about that fella, we will.

Deputy What's this about?

Woman You gotta sign it.

Deputy Why have I gotta sign it?

Woman You gotta.

Deputy Why have I gotta, then?

Woman To say that we don't have a criminal record.

Deputy You don't have a criminal record.

Woman I know.

Deputy So why have I got to sign it?

Woman To say we don't.

Deputy This is a County form.

Woman That's right.

Deputy This is an application to open a child-minding facility.

Woman That's right.

Deputy Who's opening a child-minding facility?

Woman We have no choice.

Deputy Why are you opening a child-minding facility for?

Woman Cos you've given us no choice.
  Now you gotta sign it.

Deputy Warm milk is what you need.
  You gotta get some sleep.
  There's no need for this . . .
  This . . .
  You need a good sleep.
  This is Iowa.
  Where you going to run a child-minding facility out of anyway?

37

Woman Gonna be run out of our home.
  That's the point.

Deputy You going to run a child-minding facility out of your home?

Woman That's the point.

Deputy Who you gonna get to mind?

Woman There's our two.

Deputy That's two.

Woman And Sylvia from in back.
  She's got three.
  Harriet from down by the intersection has one.
  And the Walker folks from by the church.
  And Beth and Frank's four.

Deputy That's a lot of kids.

Woman Sure is.

Deputy And who's going to do the minding?

Woman I am.
  We are.
  We all are.

Deputy All?

Woman We got to feel safe in our homes.
  That fella's front door is no more than fifty feet from ours.

Deputy We know where he lives.

Woman And we know the law.

Deputy You know that once you have gone and made yourself a registered child-minding facility –

Woman He has to move.
  Can't be closer than two thousand feet.

That's the law.
Schools, parks, malls, playgrounds, child-minding
facilities.
You got a pen?

Deputy I got a pen.

Woman I'm double-parked is all.

Deputy You don't need a pen.
You need a good night's sleep / is what you need.

Woman (*overlapping*) I'll talk to the sheriff then.
—

Deputy (*to A. G.*) You hand me a pen there.

A. G. Excuse me?

Deputy You hand me a . . .
There.
That's it.
There.

Woman You gotta sign there.

Deputy Here?

Woman There.

A. G. hands him a pen.

Deputy Here.

Woman There and . . .
There.

Deputy Here?

Woman And there.

He signs.

(*To A. G.*) Nice day for it.

A. G. Excuse me?

Woman Hot, though.

A. G. It's August.

Woman I know you?

A. G. Just moved back.

Woman Welcome back, then.

The Deputy finishes signing. He pockets the pen.

Deputy Here.

Woman (*to Deputy*) You should come down to church.

Deputy I come to church.

Woman We're short men in the choir.

Deputy I don't sing.

Woman All of you men are the same.
Think singing is for girls.

Deputy I don't.
I just don't, that's all.

Woman It's not . . . you know.
Men sing.
Men sing all the time.
You should come down.
We need men.

Deputy You need a good night's sleep if you ask me.

Woman Well I'm not.
And you got ink all over your shirt anyway.

Deputy What?

Woman Look like you been shot through the chest.

Deputy / What the?

Woman (*overlapping*) Ink.
From the pen.
Must have been leaky.

Deputy What?
I got ink all over.
I got . . .
What?
What you go and hand me a leaky pen for?
/ What?
What you?
What?
Are you trying?
Did you do that on purpose or something?
You trying to make me look like this on purpose or
something?
You trying to make me look stupid or something?

A. G. (*overlapping*) You asked me to.
I'm not trying to.
It must have been the pen.

Woman (*also overlapping*) He didn't do it on purpose.

Deputy . . . I got ink all over.

Woman You won't get that out either.
Shirt's ruined.

Deputy Hear that?
Shirt's ruined.
You hear that?
You stupid or something?
/ What did you go and hand me a leaky pen for?

Woman (*overlapping*) Don't know why you're shouting
at him.

Deputy This shirt's ruined now.
How you like it if I come over there to you and pour
ink all over your shirt then?
/ How would you like that?

A. G. (*overlapping*) I wouldn't like it much.

41

Woman You look like you've been shot.

Deputy He handed me a leaky pen is why!
Jesus!
It's everywhere.
Jesus!

Woman What are you shouting at him for?
You were the one asked for the pen.

Deputy Did I ask for a leaky pen?
Did I?
Did I say 'Can you pass me that leaky pen over there?'
This . . .
This shirt's ruined.

Woman Nothing gonna get that out.

Deputy Hear that?

Woman You should stop yelling at him.
Have a doughnut.

Deputy No!

Woman Suit yourself.
I'm double-parked.

Deputy I'm off of them is all. (*Doughnuts.*)
I gotta . . .
I gotta . . .
Jesus!

Woman You want me to leave the doughnuts?

Deputy What?

Woman Doughnuts.
You want me to leave?

Deputy Yeah, yeah.
Jesus.

Woman And you stop shouting at him.
Don't you let him shout at you like that.

A. G. / It's alright.

Deputy (*overlapping*) He handed me . . .

Woman (*also overlapping*) I'm double-parked.

Deputy Need anything else?
Got your signature?

Woman Got it.
I'm double-parked.
(*To A. G.*) Have a nice day.
(*To Deputy.*) See you down there.

Deputy What?

Woman At the Festival.

Deputy Yeah.
No.
I'm working.

Woman Too bad.
State Senator's coming down this year.

Deputy Yeah.

Woman See you, then.
(*To A. G.*) Nice to meet you.

A. G. You too.

She leaves.

Deputy Jesus!

A. G. I'm sorry.

Deputy / Yeah.
Well.

A. G. (*overlapping*) You need salt.

Deputy What?

A. G. To get the stain out.
You need salt.

Deputy I look like I been shot in the chest.

A. G. You need salt.

Deputy I gotta get some.
Some salt?

A. G. She seemed nice enough.

Deputy Excuse me?

A. G. She.
Seemed nice enough.

Deputy Yeah.
She's nice enough.
I gotta . . .
Here.
Have a doughnut.
I gotta get some . . .
Jesus.
Give me one of those. (*Doughnuts.*)
I gotta get some salt.

Black.

A Couple of Burgers

'

Outside Eldon, Iowa. A highway restaurant. A baby is crying in a back room.

Waiter You been saved?

Deputy Give me a burger.

Waiter It worry you that you eat so much?

Deputy And another to go.

Waiter (*writing it down*) Two burgers.

Deputy With pickles.

Waiter (*writing it down*) With pickles.

Deputy What's that supposed to mean?

Waiter What?

Deputy It worry me.

Waiter It worry you that you eat so much.
    That's all.

Deputy You gotta eat.

Waiter Lord doesn't want you to get fat.

Deputy He?
    / I'm not . . .

Waiter (*overlapping*) I'm gonna loan you these tapes.
    Slimming with the Gospels.
    Lord wants you ready to run the race.

Deputy I don't run.

Waiter The race of life.

Deputy I don't run, though.

Waiter Your body's on loan.
  You know that?

Deputy And a bowl of those nuts while I wait.

Waiter You're renting your body from the Lord.
  What's he gonna do if you hand it back all fat?

Deputy Won't get my deposit back.

Waiter What?

Deputy My deposit.
  Like on a house.
  You rent.
  Never mind.
  Make it those sugar-coated ones.

Waiter I'm going to loan you those tapes.

Deputy Sure.

Waiter You go to the Festival?

Deputy I had to work.

Waiter Pastor blessed that old gothic house.

Deputy Maybe that'll keep all them tourists off of it.

Waiter People come to see the house.

Deputy See is fine.
  Not allowed to climb all over it, though.

Waiter People like to come and have their photographs
taken in front of it.
  It's a . . .
  What's it called?
  Tourist . . .
  Brings in money.
  Good for the economy.

46

Deputy Strange for a town to be known for an ugly white house.

Waiter Beats being known for nothing.

Deputy Spose.
—
   That baby's got good lungs, then.

Waiter Crying to the Lord.
   You got kids yet?

Deputy Nope.

Waiter You want 'em?

Deputy Of course.

Waiter Better get on.

Deputy Got to get a wife first.

Waiter Watch your weight you'll get a wife.

Deputy You think?

Waiter 'One thing for a woman to have something to hang on to at night, another thing for her to be drowning in fat.'
   That's what it says on them tapes.

Deputy Better lend me them tapes, then.

Waiter Makes no difference.
   If you don't get saved.
   Fat or skinny.
   You go to Hell.
   It's that simple.

Deputy I been saved.

Waiter (*derisive*) When?

Deputy I just have been that's all.

Waiter Only those who got Jesus in their hearts are going to get saved.

On the Last Day.

Deputy I've got Jesus in my heart.

Waiter You get baptised by total immersion?

Deputy What?

Waiter Dunking?

Deputy I don't think.

Waiter Total immersion.

In the river.

Or a hot tub.

Hot tub's better come winter but the river shows you mean it more.

Specially if there's ice in it.

Deputy I've got Jesus in my heart.

You don't need to go worrying about that.

Waiter I'm not the one who should be worrying.

I been saved.

Total immersion.

In the winter.

In the river.

With ice in it.

Pastor made me.

On account of.

Deputy What?

Waiter Stuff I done.

Deputy Give me a couple of shakes as well.

Strawberry.

A.G. comes in, mopping his face and hands with a handkerchief.

A. G. You're out of hand towels.

Deputy Go wait in the Prowler.

A. G. Everyone's mother gives them handkerchiefs with initials on.

Deputy That so.

A. G. That and underwear.
  'A. G.'

  Showing the handkerchief.

Embarrassing.

Deputy I'll be out in five.

  A. G. goes to go.

Waiter You been saved?
  —
  Hey!

A. G. I'm sorry?

Waiter You been saved?

A. G. I . . .

Waiter Either you have been or you haven't.

A. G. I believe in God, if that's what you . . .

Waiter Deputy here hasn't.

Deputy You go wait in the car now.

Waiter He's going straight to Hell.

Deputy I told you, I've been saved.

Waiter Hell for the Deputy here is being strung up like a pig and having a hunger that never quits and being forced to feed on sand and glass.

Deputy Where you get ideas like that?

Waiter Read the Bible lately?

Deputy I read it.

Waiter Yeah, but lately?

Deputy You get me those nuts.

Waiter Roasted over an open spit / with an apple in its mouth and basted in fat.

Deputy (*overlapping*) That's enough now.
  Make sure it's the sugar-coated ones.

Waiter Oink, oink.

  Waiter goes.

A. G. Bathroom's filthy.

Deputy That a fact.

A. G. If you want my opinion I don't think it makes any difference if you've been saved or not.

Deputy I've been saved.
  I said that.
  Now, wait in the Prowler.
  —

A. G. Thanks for stopping.

Deputy Needed to eat.

A. G. I was bursting.

Deputy Should have gone before we left the station.
  —

A. G. Ugly around here.

Deputy What?

A. G. The country.
  Flat.

Deputy Nothing wrong with flat.

A. G. Hate flat.
  Used to stand on the seats of the school bus when I was a kid to try and see over the corn.

Nothing.
Just corn and flat.
Thought I might see all the way to Chicago.

Deputy That so.

A. G. Funny.
The things you think.
You been?

Deputy Been?

A. G. To Chicago?

Deputy Prefer to stay put.

A. G. In the middle of nowhere?

Deputy This isn't nowhere.

A. G. You should go.
You'd love it.
They've got music and art in Chicago.
You like music?

Deputy I listen to the radio.

A. G. What do you listen to?

Deputy News.
Weather sometimes.
Mainly news.

A. G. What about art?
You like art?

Deputy I've got a picture on my wall of a horse being gored by a bull moose.

The Waiter comes in with a bowl of nuts.

Waiter No sugared.
I looked.
Just plain.

Deputy That's fine.

A. G. You been to Chicago?

Waiter I've been to Chicago.

A. G. Deputy here's never been.
Was telling him.
He should go.

Waiter Should.

A. G. They've got that painting in Chicago.

Waiter That?

A. G. Of the house.
The gothic house.
With the folks.
At the Art Institute.
I used to go.
When I was living there.
If I ever got homesick.
Look at the painting.
That painting . . .
The Deputy here should go see that painting.

Deputy No point of going all that way to see a painting
of a house that I can drive by any day of the week.

A. G. It's a good likeness.
You should go.
You'd like it.
You'd . . .

Deputy Here.
Have a nut.

A. G. A . . . ?

Deputy A nut.
Have a nut.

A. G. No.
  Thank you.
  I'm allergic.

Deputy To nuts?

Waiter Oh yeah.
  I heard of a fella.
  Had an allergy to strawberry.
  His throat closed up like a cat's behind.
  Couldn't yell to call for help.
  Found him dead at his kitchen table.

Deputy You like that with nuts?

A. G. I'm like that with nuts, yes.

Deputy Better not have a nut, then.

Waiter (*to A. G.*) You from Chicago, then?

Deputy How're those burgers coming?

Waiter Knew a girl in Chicago once.
  Long time ago.

Deputy Don't forget those pickles.

  Waiter goes.

(*Defensive.*) I bought something off a girl once.
  On eBay.
  She wanted three-fifty for it.
  I beat her down.
  Got it for two-eighty.
  She was a cheat.
  She was from Chicago.
  —

A. G. Where . . .
  Where are we going?

Deputy Nowhere if you don't get in that Prowler.

A. G. You're not going to dump me across the county line or something, are you?

Deputy Why would I do that?

A. G. I've heard stories.

Deputy Fairy tales.

A. G. Will I be able to go home?

Deputy Sure.

A. G. When?

Deputy Not up to me.

A. G. I'll never be able to go home, will I?

Deputy Of course you will.

A. G. How do you know?

Deputy I just do.

A. G. How do you know, though?

Deputy I've got a feeling about that sort of thing and I just know.

A. G. What?
    When they pull down that school at the bottom of the road?

   Deputy chuckles.

Deputy Now that's not going to happen, is it?
    We've got a shortage on schools as it is.
    They're not going to go and tear down a perfectly good one.

A. G. I feel ill.

Deputy You going to vomit you make sure you do it before you get in that Prowler.
    Don't want it smelling of puke.

Takes weeks to get it out.
Burns me up.

A. G. This is a mistake.
You know?
I . . .
This is not what you.
He . . .

Deputy (*defensive*) This isn't nowhere, you know.

A. G. This?

Deputy This is just . . .
This is somewhere to some folks!
World's more like this than Chicago is I reckon.
I'll be right out.

> *A. G. goes.*
> *The Deputy sits.*
> *He takes the top off a salt cellar.*
> *He tries to salt the stain on his shirt.*
> *He ends up pouring salt all over.*
> *He cleans up, sort of.*
> *Waiter comes in with a couple of burgers. One on a plate and one in a bag.*

Waiter You got salt all over.

Deputy I've got a stain on my shirt.

Waiter What you got salt all over for?
I'm going to have to clean / that up now.

Deputy (*overlapping*) I cleaned it already.
It's alright.

Waiter Eat your burger.
Jesus.
(*As he cleans up.*) Where's your friend?

Deputy He's . . .

Waiter It's good to have a gun in the place, anyway.

Deputy Who's got a gun?

Waiter You do.
  I'm gonna get a gun.

Deputy Better learn how to shoot one first.

Waiter Pull the trigger.

Deputy More to it than that.

Waiter I'll get some lessons.

Deputy That so.

Waiter You wanna teach me?

Deputy No.

Waiter I was thinking of going in for the police.

Deputy That so.

Waiter Police or army.
  Army probably.
  Now I'm saved, though, Pastor going to make me an usher at church.
  He says I'm a good example of what happens after you had a white-light experience.
  I'm not sure I had one.
  I told him I had one.
  When I got baptised.
  Everything went white.
  Could have been that freezing water, though.
  Had plenty of white light experiences on weed.
  You ever smoked weed, Deputy?

Deputy I'm the Deputy.

Waiter Yeah, but . . .

Deputy Give me another bag.
  I'll take them both to go. (*Burgers.*)

Waiter You're the kind of guy who I'd like to get high with.

Would have been fun.
When I used to get high.
Love to see you high.

Deputy That's not going to happen.

A. G. You should teach me to shoot.

Deputy I . . .

Waiter You ever shot anyone?

Deputy Who am I going to shoot at out here?

Waiter Sick fuckers everywhere.

Deputy I ordered shakes too, don't forget.

Waiter Know it sounds harsh but to be honest.
That fella who got shot in the drive of the Motel 6.
Can't say I blame people.
Specially cos I got kids.
Don't spose you know anything about that, though.
Not having any kids.

Deputy I don't know anything about that.

*The Deputy is struggling to get his wallet from his
pocket.*

Waiter You keep that weight off.
Get a wife.
You'll get some kids.

Deputy How much I owe you?

Waiter Tell you what.
I'll lend you them tapes if you teach me to shoot.

*In trying to get to his wallet the Deputy sends a
shower of change from his pocket spewing across
the stage.*
    Black.

A Bed

*Outside Eldon, Iowa. The lobby of a budget motel on the
side of a highway. Fluorescent light. TV flickering in a
corner. Reception desk, perhaps behind a plate of bullet-
proof glass: when you are on the other side of it you have
to use an intercom to be heard – the effect is like
speaking from beyond a cheap electronic grave. Glass all
over the floor. A brick. A window has been broken. The
Deputy eating a burger. An eighteen-year-old male is too.*

Deputy You're doing alright then?

Eighteen-Year-Old Male What?

Deputy You're doing alright.

Eighteen-Year-Old Male Alright?

Deputy Out of this.
Situation.
Room-wise.
'No Vacancy' wise.

Eighteen-Year-Old Male You got any ketchup?

Deputy You had that sign up for months now.

Eighteen-Year-Old Male Which?

Deputy 'No Vacancy'.
Next to the Jacuzzi sign without the z's.
Seen it as I go by on the interstate.
Been like that for months.

Eighteen-Year-Old Male Hate the taste of burger with no
ketchup, Deputy.

Deputy In the bag.

Eighteen-Year-Old Male Need something wet.

Deputy Six-pack in the Prowler.

Eighteen-Year-Old Male In this heat?

Deputy I'm on duty.

Eighteen-Year-Old Male Burger's dry.

Deputy I'll get you one.

He goes.
   *As he does he passes a Resident coming into the
room with an empty toilet-paper roll.*

Excuse me.

The Resident waits.

—

*The Deputy comes in with a six-pack of beer.
   The Resident leaves.*

It's hot.

Eighteen-Year-Old Male It's August.

Deputy Still . . .
   Beer's hot.

Eighteen-Year-Old Male It's August.

Deputy I'm on duty.
   You help yourself.

He does.

So.
   That sign mean what it says?

Eighteen-Year-Old Male 'No vacancy' is 'no vacancy',
I expect.

Deputy Thought it might be broke.
Been like that a while.

Eighteen-Year-Old Male You got cigarettes?

Deputy Me?
No.

The female Manager comes in.

Manager Shit on the mattress in 22.
And something that looks like blood.

Eighteen-Year-Old Male Deputy's here.

Manager Where'd you get that beer?

Eighteen-Year-Old Male Deputy.

Deputy I . . .
You want one?

Manager Don't drink beer.

Deputy They're hot.

Manager Don't drink hot beer.
You bring me a burger or what?

Deputy I . . .
I thought you weren't . . .
He said you weren't.
You want my pickle?

Manager Thought you liked pickles.

Deputy I do but you can have it.

Manager Thanks, then.

She takes his pickle and eats it through the following.

(*To Eighteen-Year-Old Male.*) You can burn these. (*The sheets.*)
Just don't breath in the fumes when you do.

Eighteen-Year-Old Male You too good to me.

Manager Just like your momma.

Eighteen-Year-Old Male Thanks for the burger, Deputy.

Deputy It's . . .

Eighteen-Year-Old Male Sweet of you.

Deputy It's . . .
You're welcome.

Eighteen-Year-Old Male I'll know to ask for your pickle.
Next time.

Deputy Yes.
You.
I normally . . .
Yes.

Eighteen-Year-Old Male takes the sheets and leaves.

Deputy He's young.
To be working.

Manager Never too young to start work.

Deputy Here.
Working here, I mean.

Manager He lives here. /
Minds the counter.

Deputy (*overlapping*) He lives here?

Manager Yep.

Deputy He's young.

Manager What's wrong with that?

Deputy He's young is all.

Manager Old enough to vote.
Just too old to fuck his fifteen-year-old girlfriend.

Deputy What?

Manager You worried for him?

Deputy Me?
No.
He's just young.

Manager Evicted from his momma's place in Cedar Rapids.
Live next to a McDonald's.

Deputy What'd he do?

Manager I don't ask.

Deputy Better that way.

Manager Did it with his girlfriend.
Her daddy had him on statutory rape.

Deputy Know a lot for a person who doesn't ask.

Manager Keep on having to stop him from sniffing gas and playing cat and mouse with the big-rigs on the highway.

Deputy He sniffing gas?

Manager High as Jesus.

Deputy That's against the law.

Manager You think I'm running some child-minding facility here, Hallsy?

Deputy We got all this under control, you know.
No need to be concerned.

The Manager giggles.

What's so funny?

Manager It's not me who should be concerned here.

Deputy No one should / be concerned.

Manager (*overlapping*) It's them.

Deputy Them?

Manager After me, it's the back of an abandoned car behind the Dairy Queen on the I-80.

Deputy They give you trouble, you call me up.

Manager They're no trouble to me.
  I'm a woman.

Deputy What's that got to do with anything?

Manager They're terrified of me.
  Makes me laugh.

Deputy That's crazy.

Manager There's this one.
  Real fruity.
  Gets me to buy him depilatory cream when I'm in town.
  You know what depilatory cream is?

Deputy Yes.
  No.

Manager For getting rid of hair.
  He hates hair.
  Body hair.
  Specially his own.
  That's why they scared of me.

Deputy Cos of body hair?

Manager Cos I'm a woman.
  I got plenty of hair.

Deputy That so.

Manager Cept when I wax.
  Then I'm like a little mousie.

Deputy That so.

Manager Squeak, squeak.

—

Plus.
We got a girl.

Deputy What?

Manager Waits for the school bus.
Across the highway.
Belongs to that farmhouse on the other side.
Sends them scuttling like bugs.

Deputy They giving her trouble?

Manager They're terrified.

Deputy What's a kid gonna do?

Manager It's their own heads.
They're scared of their own thinking.

Deputy Whoever heard of that?

Manager She comes out.
Waits for the bus.
All you hear is the sound of men scrambling over
gravel to get inside their rooms and shut their doors.
It's awesome.

Deputy Spose that's a good thing.

Manager I had my way?
I'd drown them.
Like cats you don't want.

Deputy I like animals.

Manager You still picking up live road kill from the side
of the interstate?

Deputy Sometimes.
I might see a dog or a cat sometime.

Injured.

Or just lost on account of people not wanting them and bringing them out here into nowhere to dump.

Sheriff's made me stop.

Had the station looking like a petting zoo.

He said.

Stunk the Prowler out too.

Manager These folks here worse than animals.

Deputy Still.

Good for business.

Manager Damn straight.

Haven't had an empty room since that law got brought in.

I'm saving up to get out of here and open up a franchise selling hot tubs.

You gotta hot tub?

Deputy You know I live above a store.

Manager Ever want to get yourself a hot tub, you know where to come.

After I got that franchise.

Deputy Don't you get worried about all that warm water with everyone's dead skin and such in it all milling around together?

Manager That's what you got chlorine for, you dope.

Kills all that stuff from other people.

Deputy I don't think hot tub's my speed.

Manager Pity.

Another winter like the last and I can kiss this dump goodbye.

Deputy You look like you had trouble here, then. (*The broken window all over the floor.*)

Manager Just kids.

Throwing stones.

Breaking windows.

We don't need the Deputy showing up over it or anything like that.

Deputy I'll send someone out. /

Take a look around.

Manager (*overlapping*) We don't need you here playing Deputy, Hallsy.

Deputy I am the Deputy.

Manager You're just Hallsy.

Deputy It's wrong of these kids to cause this damage is all. /

I'll send someone out.

Manager (*overlapping*) You just here to eat burgers and watch TV, then?

Deputy Yeah.

No.

You got a room is all.

A bed?

Manager You read the sign out front?

Deputy Thought it might be wrong.

Manager Sign's not wrong.

Deputy Been like that a while.

Manager We full up.

Deputy How about the sofa?

Manager I'm not having some pervert sleeping on my sofa.

Deputy He wouldn't mind.

Manager He?
   You got someone in the back of that Prowler in this heat?

Deputy I left the window down a crack.

Manager Try the Laz-y-By.

Deputy Full up.

Manager Try the Plains.

Deputy Playground's next door.

Manager Looks like it's the truck stop on the I-80.

Deputy He could sleep on the sofa.

Manager Isn't a hostel.

Deputy I could make you take him.

Manager That'd be a first.

Deputy I could / if I wanted to.

Manager (*overlapping*) I need it quiet here.

Deputy / I like quiet.

Manager (*overlapping*) So you understand.

Deputy Spose.

Manager One more winter like the last and I'm sitting pretty in hot tubs, you understand?

Deputy I understand.
—
   I *could* make you though.

   He kicks a piece of broken glass.

Wrong of these kids. /
   I'll send someone.

67

Manager (*overlapping*) Heard they got a new Chinese
restaurant opening in Eldon anyway.

—

Run by a guy from Bermuda.
You like Chinese?

Deputy Not much.

Manager I love all that food from other places.
I order in Mexican sometimes.
Gotta go pick it up, though.
They won't come out this far.
Faggots.

Deputy Yeah.

Manager You could take me to that restaurant some time.

Deputy I could.

Manager How would that be?
Give me a chance to dress up.
Would you like that?
Me and you at a restaurant?
I always did think you were pretty.

Deputy I . . .

Manager For a police that is.

—

Deputy I'll take you to that restaurant some time, then.

Manager Thanks for the pickle, Hallsy.

Deputy You're welcome.

The Resident comes in with the empty toilet-paper roll.

Resident Toilet paper.

Manager Yeah?

Resident Ever think of leaving it when you do the rooms?

68

Manager Want chocolates on your pillow, baby, try the Holiday Inn.

Resident Maybe I will.

Manager Here. (*Toilet roll.*)

Resident You been in town this morning?

Manager You know I have.

Resident You got mail?

Manager What room you in again, hon?

Resident Same as last seven weeks.

Manager You better remind me.

Resident Twelve.

Manager Wait on.

Resident (*to Deputy*) Hot.

Deputy It's August.

Resident All month.

Manager One for you. (*A letter.*)
That's two dollars.

Resident Two?

Manager Cost of gas into town.

Resident You trying to rob me?

Manager For you.
Cos you're pretty and my favourite.
I'll give it to you for free.

Resident Gotta cheek.

Manager Try getting service like that at the Holiday Inn.

She hands him the envelope. Are they flirting?

Resident Gonna get yourself spanked.

Deputy Thank you.

Resident Excuse me?

Deputy Thank you.
—

Manager You can give me a call about that / restaurant then, Deputy.

Deputy (*overlapping*) Thank you is all.
To the lady here.

Manager / Lady?

Resident (*overlapping*) Trouble with a leaky pen, Deputy?

Deputy No.

Resident You here about those kids breaking windows?

Manager Deputy's on a social call. /
Aren't you, Deputy?

Resident (*overlapping*) Someone should do something about those kids.

Manager / Deputy's taking me out.

Resident (*overlapping*) How you think it looks, glass and shit all over the place?

Deputy You don't like it?
You clean it up.

Resident / It's not my job to do it.

Manager (*overlapping*) I'm on to it, I'm on to it.

Deputy (*to Manager*) You gonna let this . . .
Him.
Tell you.

Manager Should have / done it.

Resident (*overlapping*) Should have.

> *The Manager begins to clean up the broken glass.*
> *The Resident takes out a cigarette and a lighter.*

(*To Manager.*) You gonna get that air conditioning fixed?
—
   Hey.

Manager Excuse me?

Resident You advertise air conditioning.

Deputy You gonna . . .

Resident Yes?

Manager You wanna give me a hand here, Deputy?

Resident Cigarette?

Deputy No.
   Thank you.

Resident Here's something.
   See this? (*The lighter.*)

Deputy That?

Manager / You watch this.
   It'll make you laugh.

Resident (*overlapping*) Look.
   Now you jiggle it.
   See?
   She does the hula and takes her bikini off.

Deputy / Where'd you get that?

Manager (*overlapping*) You gotta laugh.

Resident Why?
   You want one?

Deputy Not from around here / that's for sure.

Resident (*overlapping*) It was a gift.

Deputy A gift?

Resident From a friend.

Deputy A friend?

Resident She bought it for me with her allowance.

Deputy She?

Manager People buy people gifts you know.

Deputy There's a smell in here.

Manager / It's those dirty sheets.

Resident (*overlapping*) You wanna smell at something good?
  You take a whiff of this, Deputy. (*The envelope.*)

  Deputy pulls away.

Don't you like the smell of perfume?

Deputy What's that? (*Envelope.*)

Resident Deputy doesn't like the smell / of perfume.

Deputy (*overlapping*) I like it alright.

Resident (*to Manager*) You better remember that for your big date.

Manager / Going to that Chinese.
  Just opened.
  You been?

Deputy (*overlapping*) I asked.
  I said.
  What is that?

Resident This?

Deputy That.
That.
Yes.
What is that?

Resident What is this?

Deputy That.
Yes.

Resident It's a love letter.

Deputy A . . . ?

Resident Cruel not to answer them.

Deputy Are you?

Resident Yes?

Deputy You got a death wish or something?

Manager Deputy's got no sense of humour.

Deputy I . . . . . .

Manager Never did have.
Can't tell the difference between serious and a joke.
That's what people say.

Deputy / No one says.

Manager (*overlapping*) It's a joke, Hallsy.
A joke.
You gotta . . .

Resident / Lighten up.

Manager (*overlapping*) For God's . . .
It's funny, it's funny.
It's a joke, for God's sake.
Look at him standing there like some sort of . . .
Mouth open.
It's a joke.

Resident (*referring to the envelope*) Eleven's a magical age.

Deputy What's that supposed to mean? /
  'Eleven's a magical . . .'

Resident (*overlapping*) Just is, that's all.

Manager Shit!

Deputy What?

Manager Cut myself.
  Fucking . . .

Resident You should run that under some water.

Manager Stings.
  Shit.
  I gotta get something.
  Shit.

  She leaves the room.

Deputy You better watch you don't get yourself thrown out.
  Or worse.

Resident Worse than here?

Deputy The back seat of an abandoned Buick behind the Dairy Queen.

Resident That's luxury compared to here.

Deputy Well, you feel free to go get yourself off over there.

Resident Least I'd have somewhere to bring friends.
  Can't bring anyone here.

Deputy / Who you bringing back here?

Resident (*overlapping*) Should have seen where I lived before.

74

Nice.
Hot and cold running.
Here?
Water's cold and most of the windows been smashed through.

Deputy Who is it you're bringing back here?

Resident Just saying if I wanted to.
I pay.
And if I wanted to.
Look at it.
I mean it's embarrassing.
Those sad-looking losers hanging outside their rooms looking like they're waiting for a good meal or something.

Deputy Who is it you're bringing back here?

Resident Just saying is all.

Deputy You'll end up getting killed.

Resident Like that fella at the Motel 6?

Deputy Just like him.

Resident You heard that story of the Pied Piper, Deputy?

Deputy No.

Resident He was just like him.

Deputy He?

Resident That fella at the Motel 6.
So folks say.
Good with kids.

Is the Resident fanning himself with the envelope?

—

The Deputy snatches the envelope from the Resident.

Resident / Hey, hey, hey, hey, hey!

Deputy (*overlapping*) What is this?
  What's?

Resident Told you.
  It's a letter.

Deputy What is?
  What's?

The Manager comes in with a piece of bloody tissue paper wrapped around her finger.

Manager What's going . . .?

The Deputy tears open the envelope and takes out a flattened-out cigarette packet with writing on it.

Manager / Hey!
  You can't just . . .

Deputy (*overlapping*) What's this? (*The flattened-out cigarette packet.*)

Resident (*also overlapping*) That's my property!

Deputy / What is this?

Resident It's a flattened-out cigarette pack.
  What it look like?

Manager / Hallsy, you . . .

Deputy (*overlapping*) What is . . .?

Resident (*also overlapping*)) It's a flattened-out cigarette pack.

Deputy What's it doing in there, then?

Resident Just there.

Deputy There?

Resident Inside the envelope.

Deputy From a girl?

Resident / It's for me.

Deputy (*overlapping*) Is that some girl writing to you?

Resident You jealous?

Deputy Of you?

Manager / He's joking.
  It's a joke.

Resident (*overlapping*) Some girl's writing to me.

Deputy Why is some girl writing to you?

Resident Just is.

Deputy On the back of a flattened-out cigarette pack.

Resident It's a contract.

Deputy What's a contract?

Resident None of your business.

Deputy What are you laughing at?

  The Resident is laughing.

Manager You stupid? /
  Can't you take a joke?
  It's a joke for Christ's . . .

  The Manager tries to wrestle the cigarette packet from the Deputy's hand.

Deputy (*overlapping*) This your writing?

Resident Hasn't she got a pretty hand?

Deputy (*reading*) 'One.' /
  'You need to buy me a cheeseburger every time we meet.'

Manager (*overlapping*) You gotta go now, Deputy.

Resident (*also overlapping*) That's my property.

Deputy / 'Two. You need to spend at least fifty cents on me every time.'

Resident (*overlapping*) He's taken my property.
  You are a witness here.

Manager (*also overlapping*) I'll call you about that Chinese.

Deputy / 'Three. You got to let me have at least two cigarettes when we go to bed.'

Resident (*overlapping*) I'm putting in a complaint.

Manager (*also overlapping*) You any good with them chopsticks?
  I'm no good with chopsticks.

Deputy 'Four.
  You're not allowed to touch me.
  Only when I say so.'
  —
  What is this?

Resident Told you.

Deputy Tell me again.

Resident It's a / contract.

Deputy (*overlapping*) What's a contract for?

Resident None of your business.
  Between me and my friend.

Deputy / You gonna get killed.

Manager (*overlapping*) You give that back now.

Resident (*also overlapping*) You know, Deputy.
  Most of these fellas here?

Deputy Sick!

Resident Most of these fellas don't need a therapist.
They just need a good travel agent. /
Philippines.
They know how to treat you with respect.
Or Thailand.
That's a country . . .

Deputy (*overlapping*) Showing this . . .
Pushing this . . .
Flapping it about.
Here.
In front of my face?

Manager You gonna drive me crazy.
I told you we don't need the Deputy here.
I told you that.
I'm gonna go mad.

Resident How old's the girl in your fantasies, Deputy?!
How old?
The one you jack yourself off to inside your head.
Fifteen?
Fourteen?
Eleven?
Just as well we can't see inside your head, isn't it,
Deputy?
Just as well we can't see inside a lot of heads.
How many folks you have to evict then, Deputy?
—

*And just when something might really break –
The Deputy leaves.*

This place makes me wanna hurl.

Manager This has never happened. /
I promise.
It's quiet here.
Normally.

We've never had anything like this.
He's dumb as . . .
You don't want to go and worry.
Here.
Tell you what.
I'll get you your letters for free now.

Resident (*overlapping*) Bad for you when I start telling people that this place like paying for sleeping on the street.
You better get that 'Vacancy' sign ready.
Cos you're going to need it.
There's a network, you know.

Deputy comes back in dragging A. G. behind him. A. G. has a small bag.

Deputy They got no rooms!
You're gonna sleep here! (*A sofa maybe?*)

A. G. / There's glass all over!
I can't sleep . . .!

Manager (*overlapping*) Hey!
I said . . .!
You crazy, Hallsy?

Resident (*also overlapping*) Another one for the dung heap.

Deputy / Then you better clean it up!
Go on!
You can start cleaning it up!

Perhaps A. G. begins to tentatively pick up the glass?

Resident (*overlapping*) I'm putting in a complaint here!
I have been harassed here by this man.

Manager (*also overlapping*) Hey!
You can't just . . .
He can't . . .

Deputy I'll call you. /
Bout that Chinese.
You can wear a nice dress.

He leaves.

Manager (*overlapping*) Hey!
Hey!
He can't just sleep here!
This.
He can't.
Crazy fucking fucked-up fucker!
There's no room at the inn!
You stupid-looking son of a bitch!
If you think I'd go out with you, you got another thing
coming at you!
You're stupid!
Everyone says!
Dopey-looking, stupid fucking . . .!
Jesus.
—

(*To A. G.*) What are you looking at?

Resident Fucker stole my lighter.

Black.

A Mugshot

*Outskirts of Eldon, Iowa. A child's bedroom in a
farmhouse on a highway. A window that looks out onto
corn as far as the eye can see and, in the distance, a budget
motel on the highway's edge. The walls of the bedroom
are covered in photocopied black and white mugshots of
sex offenders. The Deputy has a plate of cookies.*

Girl You can sit on my bed if you want.

Deputy No.
  I'll stand.

Girl Suit yourself.

—

Deputy You wanna cookie?

Girl You go.

Deputy Your mother thought . . .

Girl You go.

Deputy I'm not that hungry.

Girl Suit yourself.

Deputy Maybe one.

  He eats.

You got a My Little Pony.

—

  And a Barbie.

—

  I used to have Star Wars figurines.
  When I was a kid.

Girl You still got 'em?

Deputy You got a nice view.

Girl Just corn.

Deputy You can see all the way to the highway.

Girl Just a highway.

Deputy When I was in school I went to camp in Canada.
It's very green.
I missed the corn.
I like yellow.
You like yellow?

Girl You a Deputy, right?

Deputy You know I am.

Girl Your daddy was a Deputy?

Deputy That's right.

Girl You bothered that kids chuck stones at you?

Deputy They just having fun.

Girl What's the best thing about being Deputy?

Deputy Best thing?
Well.
You get free doughnuts at Jerry's when you're in uniform.
Spose that's a good thing.
And going fast in the Prowler with the siren on.
Sometimes I just do it.
For fun.
On a stretch of highway or something.
For fun.
Don't you tell anyone I told you that.

Girl What's the worse thing?

Deputy About being Deputy?

The paperwork or . . .
Telling folks that someone's died on the highway.
Or.

Girl How do you do it?

Deputy Do what?

Girl Tell folks that someone's died on the highway.

Deputy You just do.

Girl Show me.

Deputy What?

Girl I'll be the folks.

Deputy Well.
  I . . .

Girl You can put the plate on my bed.

Deputy Well.

Girl So you come to my door and you ring the bell and you'd say.

Deputy Well.
  I might say.
  You so and so?

Girl Yes.
  I'm so and so.

Deputy What?

Girl I'm being so and so.

Deputy Well, I'd say, I need to see some ID.

Girl It's in my purse.

Deputy I might ask if I can come in.

Girl I'd rather you didn't.
  I just got the rug done.

Wait here.
—
Here you are.

Deputy Then I'd say something like.
You know your son or daughter or father or whatnot, well, he just died on the highway.
I'm sorry.

Girl Then what happens?

Deputy They normally thank me.

Girl They thank you?

Deputy Specially if I come a long way out of town.
Sometimes they invite me in for coffee or a sandwich.

Girl They invite you in?

Deputy If it's a long way.
Once a woman screamed.
Her husband shook her.
They didn't invite me in.
You wanna be a Deputy?

Girl I'm gonna be Sheriff.

Deputy You'd be my boss then.
You'd get free doughnuts then at Jerry's then.
Even out of uniform.

Girl Can I see your badge?

Deputy OK.
I guess.

He takes it off and gives it to her.

Girl It's heavy.

Deputy It's metal.

Girl Can I put it on?

Deputy OK.

Girl Can you . . . ?

Deputy Don't you move now. (*Pinning the badge.*)
I don't wanna open a vein.
There.
You'd get free doughnuts at Jerry's now.
—
Your mother said I should come on up.
She said I'd be impressed.
You got quite a set-up here. (*The mugshots.*)
You be careful that all these faces don't go and give you nightmares now.

Girl Sometimes I dream they come into my room.

Deputy You see?
These mugshots giving you nightmares.
You shouldn't worry.
We got everything under control.
—
Barbie could take a ride on My Little Pony's back.

Does he make Barbie take a ride on My Little Pony's back?

—

Your Momma thought you might want this.

He takes a mugshot of A. G. from his pocket.

It's the latest.
Just moved into the motel across the highway.
I don't want to go frightening you or nothing, but you know I gotta bring these round by law.

Girl He looks sad.

Deputy Hadn't noticed.

Girl His ears are too big for his head.

Deputy Your ears keep growing.
And your nose.

Girl Some of them are ugly.

Deputy I don't . . .

Girl That one's sweet-looking. (*One on the wall.*)

Deputy Which one?

Girl This one looks like he doesn't know which end is up. (*The one in her hand.*)

Deputy He plays piano.

Girl He's a child-molester.
　You gonna put it up for me?

Deputy I can't reach.

Girl You can stand on my bed.

Deputy That what your momma does?

Girl No.

Deputy You got tape?

Girl Here.

Deputy You gonna run out of space.

　He puts the mugshot up.

You're gonna have to find a new interest then.
　You like horses?

Girl You know eight in ten still live at home?

Deputy What?

Girl You know nine in ten been refused military service?

Deputy That a fact.

Girl First thing you know is they want to be friends with your family.
　With your parents.
　Then they buy you stuff.
　They're always nice, laughing at your jokes and stuff.

Deputy Where you get all this talk from?

Girl My momma and I are putting together a profile for the church webpage.
A profile of the Wapello County sex-offender.
There's common denominators, you know.

Deputy That a fact.
There.
How's that? (*The mugshot.*)

Girl One came up here / the other day.

Deputy (*overlapping*) Up here?

Girl Bold as brass.
From the motel.
See that glass?
He drank out of it.

Deputy Your Momma know about this?

Girl He was looking for work.
Momma was at the Go Through.
I told him we didn't have any work.
He looked thirsty so I gave him a drink.

Deputy You know you shouldn't be playing like that with fire.

Girl Jesus would have given him a drink.

Deputy Well.
You ain't Jesus.
You shouldn't be entertaining these men.
They down there in that motel for a reason.

Girl He was eighteen.
Said he lived with his parents in Cedar Rapids.

Deputy You gotta promise me no more entertaining strangers up here.

88

Girl I got nothing to worry about.
  I'm almost safe.
  I almost got a chest.
  This glass got his DNA on it.

Deputy I don't know anything about that.

Girl It does.

Deputy I'd give that glass a good wash if I were you.

Girl I'm keeping it.
  He was a good sport.

Deputy Sport?

Girl He didn't flinch.
  When I hit him.

Deputy You hit him?

Girl I chucked a stone at him as he walked back down the drive.
  Hit him in the shoulder.
  Didn't flinch.
  Just turned and smiled and waved.
  Like this.

Deputy You shouldn't be throwing rocks at no one.

Girl They only end up down there cos you evict them.

Deputy It's for the best.

Girl How do you do it?

Deputy Do what?

Girl Evict them.

Deputy I . . .
  I.
  I go to their homes and I hand them the papers.

Girl That it?

Deputy Yep.

Girl What happens when you hand them the papers?

Deputy When . . .

Girl Say you've just handed me the papers.

Deputy You.

Girl I got 'em in my hand.
I'm looking at them.

Deputy I'd say.

Girl Yeah?

Deputy I'd say.
You're evicted.
You got such-and-such time to leave the premises.

Girl What if I don't?

Deputy You?

Girl I'm being them.

Deputy You.
Well.
We'd come and make you.
Them.
We'd make them leave by force.

Girl You had to do that?

Deputy You got other interests?
What about ballet?
Dancing?
Stories?
You like stories?
You know the story of the Pied Piper?

Girl Everyone knows that one.

Deputy I don't.

Girl A person.

He's a piper.
He rids the town of a rat plague by playing his pipe
and having all the rats follow him and then drowning
them in the river.

Deputy Rats aren't so bad.

Girl But . . . the adults don't pay the piper for drowning
all the rats in the river . . . so . . . the piper takes all the
children away.
To punish the adults.
They're devastated.
What would be better, do you think, to live in a town
knowing that your parent was a cheat because she
cheated the piper out of his money?
Or to go away with the piper never to see your parent
again?

Deputy I don't . . .

Girl I'd rather go away.
With the piper.
Don't you think?
The piper would be more fun and he knows how to
deal with rats.

Deputy How about singing?
You like singing?

Girl
'I remember Daddy's hands how they held my momma
    tight,
And patted my back for something done right.
There are things that I've forgotten that I loved about
    the man
But I'll always remember the love in Daddy's hands.

Daddy's hands were soft and kind when I was cryin,
Daddy's hands were hard as steel when I'd done wrong,
Daddy's hands weren't always gentle but I've come to
    understand,

There was always love in Daddy's hands.'
—

Deputy You gonna give me back that badge now?

Girl You still play with those Star Wars figurines.

Deputy What?

Girl You still play with those Star Wars figurines?
At night?

Deputy Now you take that badge off.

Girl My momma says I can see through people.
To the core.
Then I speak the truth.

Deputy It's good to tell the truth.

Girl Who's your favourite?

Deputy I don't . . .

Girl Luke?
Han Solo?

Deputy You should be playing with your Barbie.

Girl You don't know much.
For a Deputy.

Deputy Don't you be rude.

Girl I bet if I came to your house I'd find all of those
figurines displayed nice along your mantle.

Deputy I don't have a fireplace.

Girl By your bed then.

Deputy My . . .

Girl You like those perverts?

Deputy Those . . .

Girl You drive around with them in your car.

Deputy How else I gonna get around?

Girl You talk to them.

Deputy To be civil.

Girl You eat with them.

Deputy I never.
  Here!
  You take Barbie here.
  You take her.
  Here.
  You should be playing with her.
  Like this.
  You should be playing with her and with My Little
Pony.
  Like this.
  See?
  Now.
  You go and give me back that badge.

  She takes it off.

That's the way.

  She licks the badge.

Deputy What'd you go and do that for?
  What you want to go and lick that badge for?
  You gotta be full of the things that little girls is full of.
  Like sugar and spice and such.
  Alright?
  You gotta play with your Barbie and sing songs.
  Now you give me back that badge.
  Please.
  Here.
  Give me . . .
  Give . . .
  Give me that.

Now don't you be naughty now.
Give!

In an attempt to get the badge he pushes her quite hard.
    She falls to the floor.
    A moment of shock.
    She starts to weep quietly.

Now.
    Now don't . . .
    Don't you . . .
    I said . . .
    I told you to give it . . .
    I told . . .
    Now you stop.
    You don't want your momma . . .
    Here.
    Here.

Girl I'm scared.

Deputy You're . . . ?

He takes the trick lighter out of his pocket.

Here.
    See this?
    You look at this.
    You don't need to . . .
    You stop now.
    You stop that crying now.
    Here.
    See?
    Look.
    You jiggle the lady and . . .
    See?
    See?
    It's funny.
    It's fun.

See?
She's a funny lady.
See?

Is there laughter through the tears?

That's it.
And sing.
You could sing too.

'I remember Daddy's hands how they held my momma
tight –'

You sing now.

The girl joins in through the tears.

Deputy *and* **Girl**
'And patted my back for something done right.
There are things that I've forgotten that I loved about
the man
But I'll always remember the love in Daddy's hands.'

Girl
/ 'Daddy's hands were soft and kind when I was cryin,
Daddy's hands were hard as steel when I'd done wrong,
Daddy's hands weren't always gentle but I've come to
understand,
There was always love in Daddy's hands.'

Deputy (*overlapping*) And the pretty lady dances.
See?
See her dance?
Up and down.
Up and down.

Black.
The stage bursts into flame.
The budget motel burns to the ground.

A Pair of Shoes

Outskirts of Eldon, Iowa. The highway. Corn high. Night. The sky is orange. The blue strobe from a police Prowler pulses across the stage. A. G. is trapped in a searchlight (from the Prowler). He has a cut on his face and is without his shoes. The Deputy is at a distance.

Deputy Where are your shoes?

—

You could have got killed.

—

Coming out of the corn like that onto the highway.
Trucks go fast past here, you know.
Too fast to stop.
You stupid or what?
Just standing there like a goldfish or something?
You understand me?
You come running out of the corn like that onto the highway you going to get yourself killed.
Do you understand?!
Next time it might not be me.
Next time it might be someone who wouldn't stop.
You understand?

A. G. My feet are black.

Deputy Teach you to go without shoes.

A. G. There's something on the bottom of them.

Deputy Mud probably.

A. G. Smells like blood.

Deputy I don't smell anything.

A. G. I'm afraid to look.

Deputy Should know better than to run out onto the highway at night time without your shoes.

A. G. I didn't have time.

Deputy End up as road kill.

A. G. With all the screaming.

Deputy I don't hear any screaming.

A. G. Please.

He goes to move toward the Deputy.

Deputy Stay where you are!
—
You cold or what?

A. G. I . . .

Deputy It's August for heck's sake.
What you shaking for?

A. G. I . . .

Deputy Stop shaking!

A. G. I think there's something wrong with my feet.

Deputy That's better. (*The shaking.*)
I've seen dogs shake like that.
Before they get hit.

A. G. dry-retches.
The Deputy watches.

Wanna nut?

A. G. What?

Deputy Have a nut.

A. G. I . . .

I'm allergic . . .
My feet . . .

Deputy They're sugar-coated.

A. G. No.
Thank you.

Deputy Don't know what you're missing.

A. G. There's blood on my feet.

Deputy That old motel went up like a book of matches
that's for sure.
Fire's pretty through the corn, though.
You're shaking again.

A. G. Sorry.

Deputy You ever seen a field of corn burn to the ground?

A. G. What?

Deputy My father took me to see one once.
Couldn't see the black on the road for all the creatures
running out of the corn.
Creatures that would eat each other in normal life.
Rats and mice and snakes and wild cats.
All coming out of the burning corn.
Scrambling over each other to get out.
I felt for them . . .

A. G. / Please.

Deputy (*overlapping*) You'd think the fire would have
killed them all but there they were coming out of the corn
in waves like the animals off of the Ark . . .

A. G. / Please.

Deputy (*overlapping*) There was just no killing them
creatures.
Takes more than a fire to kill some things, don't you
think?

Suddenly the Deputy chokes on a nut.
He coughs and splutters.
Through all of the coughing and spluttering he
indicates to A.G. to whack him on the back.
A.G approaches him.
A.G. whacks him on the back.
The Deputy falls to the ground.

Shit!
Went down the wrong way!
Fucking!
Coulda choked me!
Fucking nuts!
Fucking!
Last time I buy these!
Coulda killed me.

Deputy throws the bag of nuts into the corn.
The two men are closer than they've ever been.

Nasty cut.

A. G. I fell.

Deputy Clumsy.

A. G. Please.
I saw someone with his head on fire.
There was moaning.
Men crying for their mothers.
You're not going to . . .

Deputy Not going to what?

A. G. / Just leave me.
Please.
You seem like a decent . . .

Deputy (*overlapping*) I gotta get some . . .
What?
You don't know me.

A. G. Seem like.

Deputy What folks seem and what folks are is two different things.

A. G. Gentle.
Gentle. /
You seem gentle.

Deputy (*overlapping*) Gentle like a fag?

A. G. You've got a kind face.

Deputy What are you saying?

A. G. No.
I thought. /
Here's a man who would help you.
Who wouldn't leave another man.
Who'd do the right thing . . .

Deputy (*overlapping*) You're going to have to stop talking.
I'm going to pretend you're not talking.
I'm not hearing you.

A. G. . . . I'm not a criminal!
If that's what you're thinking.
If that's what's stopping you.
I'm . . .

Deputy / I know what you are.

A. G. (*overlapping*) . . . I'm not like the others.
Some of them.
They disgust me.
As much as they disgust you.
They think they're doing them a favour.
I'm not like that.
I'm like you.
I promise you.

You have to believe me.
I'll tell you the truth.
It was . . .
Me and him.
He.
My.
We.
We grew feelings.
That's all.
We had feelings.
He did too.
I didn't hurt anyone.
We grew feelings.

Deputy You heard that story of the Pied Piper?

A. G. Pied?

Deputy You heard it?

A. G. Jesus.
I read it in a children's book.
A book when I was a child.

Deputy About that piper who got rid of all these rats by playing on his pipe and having the rats follow him and drowning them in the river?

A. G. Please.

Deputy You ever wonder what happens if there's no river?

A. G. What?

Deputy What happens if that town's like Katchetaw or Jackson and they don't have a river?

A. G. I'm not?

Deputy How's he going to kill all those rats then?

A. G. I'm not . . . ?

Deputy If he's got no river to drown them in?

A. G. I'm not following . . .

Deputy What's he going to do to all those rats then?

A. G. I . . .

Deputy You seem pretty . . .
  I dunno.
  You know music and art and such.
  Thought you might know.

A. G. I don't . . .

Deputy Piper's job to drown those rats, but if there's no river?

A. G. I don't know.

  What looks like snow begins to fall.

Deputy Don't know much, do you?

A. G. You're . . .

Deputy / For someone who knows music and art.

A. G. (*overlapping*) I don't know, I don't know, I don't know, I don't know!

Deputy What's . . . ?

  The Deputy reaches for A. G.'s face and picks off a flake.

This a miracle or something? (*The snow.*)

A. G. It's ash.

Deputy For a second.
  Thought it was snowing in August.

A. G. It's the fire.

Deputy Thought it was snow.
  For a second.

A. G. It's ash.

Deputy Can't say I'm not disappointed.
  Thought it was a miracle.
  Thought it could be something that I could tell the kids
for a minute there.

A. G. It's ash.
  Please.
  From the fire.

Deputy Thought it might have been.
  You know what they talk about in church and such?
  What's it?

A. G. End days.

Deputy That's it.
  See?
  You're not so stupid after all.

A. G. Please.
  It's the fire.
  That's all.
  Ash.
  From the fire.
  Please.
  I need you to help . . .

Deputy Can I tell you something?

A. G. You?

Deputy I would cut my hands off if I thought that I might
go and touch a person.
  You know that?
  We got a shredder down the station.
  I'd do them in that.

I'd just turn it on and grit my teeth and push them on in.
Simple.
If I was ever . . .
We got to be safe, you know.
From ourselves.
I mean.
From each other.
From people.
You know what I'm talking about?

A. G. What are you going to do?

The Deputy sees something in the night sky.

Deputy Look!

A. G. You're scaring.

Deputy Shooting star.

—

You missed it.

Black.

A Phone

Outside Eldon, Iowa. The shell of the budget motel still smouldering after the fire. The Girl is dancing/playing in the ruins.

Girl How long have you been watching me?

Nan I saw you from the highway.

Girl I'm dancing.

Nan This is a dangerous place for you to be dancing.

Girl Just a burnt-out motel.

Nan You could step on a nail.

Girl I'm wearing boots.

Nan Nevertheless . . .

Girl What you doing here then?

Nan Heard there was a fire.

Girl All over the news.

Nan Thought I'd come and see for myself.

Girl You like fires?

Nan No.
   Now you be careful there.

Girl I'm always careful.

Nan Give me your hand in case I slip.

   The Girl does so.

Girl You got bony hands.

Nan You wait till you're my age.

Girl I'm never going to get bony hands like that.

Nan You wait.

Girl I know you.

Nan Do you?

Girl You're one of those dress-up people.
From the Festival every year.
From out the front of that house.

Nan Won eleven years in a row.

Girl We did a project on it in school.

Nan You go down there this year?

Girl No.

Nan Everyone was down there.

Girl It's just for kids and old people.

Nan Missed a big day.
They had a State Senator there.

Girl You got kids?

Nan I got a kid.

Girl It a boy or a girl?

Nan He's a boy.

Girl You should have bought him up here so I could play with him.

Nan He's too old to play.
You're a bit like him though.
When he was your age.

Girl I'm tall for my age.

Nan You are.

Girl He tall for his age?

Nan When you're an adult you just are the height you are.

Girl I found this. (*A toothbrush.*)

Nan You put that down.
   You don't know where it's been.

Girl It's all burnt by the fire.
   Pastor says fire's purifying.

Nan Wouldn't find me playing with someone else's old toothbrush.
   What else you find?

Girl Loads of stuff.
   A comb.
   Driver's licence.
   Picture of the President.
   Lots of stuff that used to be something but that just looks like weird stuff now cos it's all melted out of shape by the fire.

Nan Must have had some heat in it.

Girl We could feel it from our place.
   Felt like the world was on fire.

Nan You live up there?

Girl Other side of the highway.
   Look at this. (*The lighter.*)

Nan What's that?

Girl It's a lighter.
   You shake it and . . .

Nan I can't make that out.
Too small.

Girl It's a lady.
She does the hula and takes her top off.

Nan That's not a thing for a tall young lady to be playing with.

Girl I got this too. (*A mobile phone.*)

Nan You find that here?

Girl My mother gave it to me.

Nan Pretty colour.

Girl I got 911 programmed on speed dial.

Nan That so.

Girl All I have to do is press this one and the cops'd come.

Nan Clever.

Girl It takes photographs too.
Wanna see?

Nan I don't have my glasses.
Be all blurred blobs to me.

Girl You can take photographs of disasters and stuff and send them in to the news.
See? (*The phone.*)

Nan I told you I can't . . .
What is that? (*The phone.*)
A cat?

Girl That's my hamster.
And this one.

Nan What's . . . ?

Girl That's my ma at the Go Through.

Nan She looks pretty.

Girl You said you couldn't see.

Nan She's a pretty blob.

Girl This is my best friend Tabatha.
  Before she ganged up with Doxanna on me.

Nan Girls can be cruel.

Girl I don't give a shit anyway.

Nan You watch your mouth now.

Girl This is me winning third at the school swim meet.

Nan You a swimmer?

Girl Backstroke.

Nan That a fact.

Girl That's nothing. (*Scrolling through.*)
  That's nothing.
  More trees and shit.
  Sorry.
  Nothing. (*Scrolling.*)
  That's the fire. (*Finding something.*)

Nan I can see the red.

Girl It was red alright.
  Fire trucks from Ottumwa. (*Scrolling.*)
  Three of them.
  Paramedics.
  That's it from further down the road.
  There's some men. (*Another one.*)

Nan Just men?

Girl Running.
  From the flames.

Nan Can't make them out.

Girl There. (*Finding one.*)
   In the back.
   Here's another one.

Nan Another?

Girl Man.

Nan It's too small.

Girl He's all burnt up.
   And there's the same one.
   Heading off into the corn.

Nan I can't . . .
   No.
   It's no use.
   I should have brought my glasses.

Girl You could get your son to bring them up here for
you.

Nan My . . .
   I don't . . .
   He's busy.

Girl He live around here?

Nan I don't . . .
   No.

Girl What's he like then?

Nan I never thought.
   He just is like he is.

Girl I bet he was a naughty baby.
   Boys are naughty babies.

Nan He was . . .
   Happy.
   He'd grab me around the head.
   After he'd had a nap.

He'd be so excited to see me.
He'd eat my face.

Girl You win again this year?

Nan We?

Girl That Gothic Day competition.

Nan This year?
No.
This year we lost.

Girl Never mind.
It's not about win or lose.
It's how you run the race.

Nan That's true.

Girl I'm sending these pictures in to the news.

Nan Good for you.

Girl We prayed for them.
Last night.
The victims of the fire.

Nan You're a good girl.

Girl You wanna watch me pirouette?

Nan I'll watch you pirouette.

Girl You sit there.
I need to do it on something flat.
Hold these so I don't drop them. (*The phone and toothbrush and the lighter.*)

Nan I'll hold the phone.
But not those.

The Girl throws the toothbrush and lighter away.

Girl Now you watch me.

The girl runs off stage.

Can you see?

Nan I can see.

Girl (*off*) Are you sure?

Nan I can see.

Girl (*off*) Here goes.
  Make sure you look!
  Look!
  / Can you see?
  Can you see?
  I'm fast.
  See?
  Are you looking?
  Are you looking?
  Are you looking?

Nan (*overlapping*) Very good.
  Very good.
  Just like a real ballet dancer.
  Very pretty.

  She is peering at the phone desperately trying to make out the images.

I'm looking.
  I'm looking.
  I'm looking.
  Very good.

  Black.

Epilogue

Chicago. The Daniel F. and Ada L. Rice Building, Art Institute of Chicago. The painting 'American Gothic' by Grant Wood.

A. G. I forget how small it is.
  In my mind it's always . . .
  Well.
  Lifelike.
  Sized.
  —

  I didn't think you were ever going to stop.
  You know that?
  Thought you were just going to keep on driving that Prowler for ever.
  Till you ran out of gas.
  Or got to Canada.
  Most likely run out of gas first.
  We came clean across Iowa and Illinois.
  Further than you've ever been before, I reckon.

Deputy She looks too young to be his wife.

A. G. Could be his daughter.

Deputy He looks . . .
  Pissed off.

A. G. He's protecting what's his.

Deputy That so.

A. G. You like it?

Deputy Not much.
  Long way to come to see what I could see at home.

Good likeness of the house, though.
I spose.
Don't care much for the folks, though.

A. G. It's a very important painting.

Deputy Could have fooled me.

A. G. You hungry?

Deputy I'm not hungry.

A. G. You didn't eat the whole way.

Deputy Didn't feel like it.

A. G. Didn't say much either.

Deputy Like quiet.

A. G. I like talking.

Deputy Noticed.

A. G. Thanks for the bandages.

Deputy Don't thank me.
They were just there in the kit.

A. G. We can just sit here if you like.
In the quiet.
If you like.
—

A small Child comes on and looks at the painting.

A. G. Hello.

Deputy I've been thinking.

A. G. You're full of surprises, aren't you?

Deputy You making fun of me?

A. G. No.

Deputy You know that piper?

A. G. The which?

Deputy From that children's story.
   I've been thinking.
   If there was no river or water or whatnot.
   That piper just have to keep walking and keep playing
his pipe and the rats would keep following him.
   If he had nowhere to drown them.

A. G. But he did.
   He had a river.

Deputy Otherwise he'd be bound to those rats for ever.
   Playing his pipe and leading those rats.
   What's that word?

A. G. I don't think . . .

Deputy Perpetuity.
   In perpetuity.

A. G. For ever.

Deputy That town's got to be free from rats.

   The Child leaves.

Foot stinks.
   You better see to it or it'll go gangrene.
   Drop off.

   The Deputy goes to go.

A. G. I've got jelly beans.
   You want a jelly bean?

Deputy You . . .

A. G. Yes?

Deputy You make me wanna hurl.

A. G. Oh.

Deputy Just so you know.

A. G. I . . . ?
Yes.
Yes.
Absolutely.
Of course.
I . . .

Deputy Just so we're clear.

A. G. Of course.

Deputy So.
What else they got here?

A. G. Sears Tower.
They got a lake.
It's big.
Like the ocean.

Deputy Never been.

A. G. It's big.
You can't see to the other side.

Deputy I'd like to see that.

A. G.
Deputy.
Painting.
Black.